Special Parent, Special Child

*Parents of Children with
Disabilities Share
Their Trials, Triumphs,
and Hard-Won Wisdom*

T O M S U L L I V A N

A Jeremy P. Tarcher/Putnam Book
published by
G. P. Putnam's Sons
New York

Most Tarcher/Putnam books are available at special quantity discounts for bulk purchases for sales promotions, premiums, fund-raising, and educational needs. Special books or book excerpts also can be created to fit specific needs.

For details, write or telephone Special Markets, The Putnam Publishing Group, 200 Madison Avenue, New York, NY 10016; (212) 951-8891.

A Jeremy P. Tarcher/Putnam Book
Published by G. P. Putnam's Sons
Publishers Since 1838
200 Madison Avenue
New York, NY 10016

http://www.putnam.com/putnam
First Trade Paperback Edition 1996

Published simultaneously in Canada

Library of Congress Cataloging-in-Publication Data

Sullivan, Tom, date
    Special parent, special child: parents of children with disabilities share their trials, triumphs, and hard-won wisdom/Tom Sullivan.
    p.   cm.
    "A Jeremy P. Tarcher/Putnam book"
    ISBN 0-87477-830-1
    1. Parents of handicapped children.   2. Handicapped children.
    I. Title
    HQ759.913.S85   1995   94-34099 CIP
    649´ .151—dc20

Designed by Lee Fukui
Cover photograph of family by Walter Hodges/West Light
Photograph of the author © by David L. Cornwell

Printed in the United States of America
1 2 3 4 5 6 7 8 9 10

This book is printed on acid-free paper.

To my mother, Marie Sullivan, and to all mothers and fathers who turn children of disability into people of ability.

Contents

Acknowledgments

To MY MOTHER, FATHER, AND SISTERS, a family committed to the idea that I could be equal in a difficult world. Thank you.

To all the professionals who made a difference in my life.

To Billy Hannon and my other childhood friends—thank you for letting me be part of the gang.

To Jeremy and Dan, and everyone at Jeremy Tarcher Publishing, thank you for believing. Thank you for committing.

To Loretta Barrett, a woman who doesn't agent books as much as she is an agent for creative, loving ideas.

To Susan Golant; you forced me to find accurate expression for ideas and emotions within the body of this work. I am very grateful.

To Marjorie, and the ladies of E.D.A.; you provided hard work and eyes that gave me vision to complete this loving task. Thank you for all you do to fulfill my creative need.

To Patty; thank you for keeping our lives together and our love in balance while I sought to find the truth in the lives of our special parents.

To Nick and Lindy, Robin and Bob, Diana, Arthur and Karen, Cheri and David, and Jim and Anita, my special friends who allowed me to enter their special lives—I hope I have not abused the privilege. The effort was made with absolute love and absolute commitment.

To the children of our special families; may you come to understand the love and commitment of all of your parents. Thank you for shedding light on the issues confronting all children of disability throughout the world.

Different Rainbows

LOIS HARRELL, 1993

I saw the baby's eyes.
I heard the parents' sighs.
I hoped for otherwise.
But he will not see.

No place to lay the blame,
Though lives no longer same,
And then the questions came.
"How will it be?"

"He will never know a rainbow; a sunset; a star.
How can we share what colors are?
And . . . and . . . and . . .
Help us understand."

In time, my friends, you'll know,
As you help your child to grow,
His is a different rainbow!
You will see!

Special Parent,
Special Child

CHAPTER

My Mother

MY MOTHER IS EIGHTY YEARS OLD, a fact that she doesn't even try to deny. Indeed, she is very proud of the way the years have treated her. Recently, my very large Boston-Irish extended family got together to throw her an eightieth birthday party that would have made St. Patrick believe the snakes had returned to Erin's Isle. It was fantastic. The shared spirits, both of the camaraderie and the Jamison's, brought out good talk, good fun, and wonderful stories (a quality fundamental to being Irish).

While dancing with my mother (she still loves to do that), I found myself telling her how much I owed her when I considered the quality of my life. I was born blind. Actually, I suppose that's not really the truth. I was born three months premature and became blind when too much oxygen was pumped into the incubator that kept me alive. My early arrival into the world was

I

probably a precursor to the rest of my life. I've always taken chances, I've always needed to be first. I've always celebrated the joy of a challenge.

And as I danced around the hall with my little Irish mother, I found myself thinking that none of the success I now enjoy would have been possible had she not been a woman of tremendous strength, commitment, and courage. And so, I took Mum off the dance floor, sat her down at one of the quiet tables in the hall, and had the most revealing talk I have ever enjoyed with this marvelous woman.

I began by telling her how proud I was to have a mother who cared so much about all of her children, but most particularly for her handicapped son.

"Oh," she said, "you were special right from the beginning. You were in such a hurry to come into this world. My pregnancy was completely normal. I don't know why you had to come early, but you did."

"You mean you had no idea that I was going to arrive three months ahead of schedule?" I laughed. "No pains? No indications?"

"Absolutely none," she said. "In fact, your father was on a trip to Florida. Your grandmother, Nana Regan, and your godmother, Anna Shehan, were at the house for dinner when I began to have labor pains."

"This was on the night of March twenty-sixth?"

"That's right," she said. "You were born early the next morning. Labor wasn't that hard at all."

"Did Dr. McDonough think I'd be okay? Did he believe I'd make it?"

"He said you were obviously small. That's why he put you in an incubator. But he thought you were tough. None of us expected you to lose as much weight as you did. You went from four pounds three ounces to three pounds four ounces in just a couple of days. They had to use a milk pump on me to keep supplying you with real mother's milk while you were in the incubator. And then, while you stayed in the hospital over the next few months, I had to have a pump at the house. Your father brought milk down to you every day."

"How long was I in the hospital?" I asked.

"Three months," she said. "We brought you home in the middle of June and the whole family turned out. All of my sisters and brothers, your cousins, your sisters Peggy and Jeanne's friends, and a lot of the people who worked for your father. You'd think the president was coming to visit or something."

"Where was this?" I asked. "What house did you bring me back to?"

"West Roxbury," she said. "You know, 14 Greaton Road."

"Did we go to Scituate for the summers back then?" I asked.

"Yes, but we didn't live in the cottage that you remember as a little boy; that came later."

"Let's see," I said, "if I was three months old when I came home, I was as developed as I would have been had you experienced a full-term pregnancy, so the issues relating to my blindness didn't show up right away."

"That's right," she said.

I knew we were getting to the first tough question. "Well, Mum, when did you start to think I might be blind?"

"During the first week of August, Tom. But I wasn't the person who figured it out. I suppose mothers are always the last to know—or admit."

"Then who brought it up for the first time, Mum?"

"It was Nana Regan," she said. "She always noticed things that the rest of us missed."

I knew that was true, because I could remember as a little

boy how my grandmother helped open the world of senses for a curious little blind child.

"What did she say?" I asked. "How did she tell you?"

"She didn't actually tell me," Mum said. "She brought it up to your father first. Then they both asked me to sit down. They thought they had some bad news to deliver. I'm sure it was tough for them to tell me what they thought, but it wasn't half as tough as it was for me to accept the idea that I had a blind child."

"Wait a minute, Mum," I said. "Don't get ahead of the story. How did they say it? Do you remember the words?"

"Not really. But I remember how awkward they were, both of them kind of stuttering and stammering, not really able to get the truth out. They never really said they were certain, but how could they be? Nobody knew for sure, so they just said they thought something might be wrong with Tommy's eyes."

"What did you do then?" I asked.

"We went to Dr. McDonough. He made an appointment with a famous eye doctor, Dr. Merrill King, of the Massachusetts General Eye and Ear Infirmary."

"What did he say?" I asked.

"I know he didn't mean any harm, Tommy. But he told us he believed you would have some light perception; you probably wouldn't be totally blind. He was sure you'd even be able to see some shadows, maybe even some large objects."

"So he created a false sense of hope," I said.

"Yes," said Mum. "It's difficult for a parent trying to understand the condition of a child, when a doctor holds out hope but there really isn't any."

I took Mum's hand. "What happened then?"

"Dr. King referred us to a very, very famous German doctor, Dr. Veerhoff, also at Massachusetts Eye and Ear. I remember that day like it was only yesterday. Your dad and I took you to see him; he looked in your eyes and without pause, or the smallest hesitation, or feeling, he said to us: 'Your son is permanently blind. I suggest you find a good institution for him.'"

I squeezed her hand a little harder. "I'm sorry, Mum," I said.

"Oh, that's all right, Tommy. But your father went crazy. He tried to fight with the doctor. He actually tried to have a fist fight with him. I know it was because he was so hurt inside."

"How did you react, Mum?" I asked.

"Oh, I got all the way home, and laid you down in your crib, and as I looked at you, I went a bit crazy. I started banging the walls and throwing things around, and asking God, 'Why me?' I'm sure that happens to every parent who has a child with a handicap. I cried and cried and kept throwing anything I could get my hands on. Jeanne told me later that I did that for hours. She was downstairs. In fact, the whole family was downstairs; none of them would dare come up to try to comfort me or talk to me. They must have known that I had to handle it alone."

"But it all worked out, Mum," I said. "I love my life today. I've done just fine."

"I know that, Tommy," she said. "I'm so proud of you. Every day I thank God that you are the way you are. But you are exceptional. We found out that you loved music, and that you had a special talent. And then, you were such a good student, and even a good athlete. I think you would have been a successful person whether you'd been sighted or blind. The blindness just made it tougher."

"I suppose that's true," I said. I know it isn't easy for kids who don't have such special gifts. "Mother," I said, "you were the most special gift I got. The way you treated me—normal, I mean, like other children. That's what made the difference; that's what made my life work."

"The hardest decisions, Tommy, were about finding the balance between protecting you and giving you the freedom I thought you needed. I realized early that we also had to allow you to live as normal a life as possible. When I hear about all the handicapped children going to normal schools today, I remember that was the hardest decision your father and I had to make about you. We chose to send you to a school for blind children. I suppose now, as I look back, it was a mistake. You would have done just fine with sighted kids."

"Oh, don't worry about that, Mum," I said. "That's all hindsight. Nobody makes all the right decisions. You did the best you could."

She laughed. "I guess that's true. Every parent has to do the best job possible. That's all anyone can do. Sometimes they're right, and sometimes they're wrong. But if they keep loving and keep trying, it usually works out." She laughed again. "Boy, this has been a pretty serious conversation in the middle of my birthday party."

"I'm sorry, Mum," I said. "I didn't mean to make it so heavy."

But throughout the rest of that day, and in subsequent ones, I thought about all the parents who have written me letters over the years asking for advice about the raising of their children with disabilities. Now I wish I had just given their letters to my mother. She obviously knows a lot more about this process than I do.

And so this book is dedicated to my mother: to her love, her patience, and commitment, along with a very large dose of guts. All essential qualities needed if a child with a handicap is going to find life, balance, and a place in the world.

A JOURNEY OF HOPE

For over twenty years, I have been a publicly visible person, on television, records, and in film. I have also been a disabled person all my life. "Celebrity" only means that you usually get a good table in a restaurant. I am constantly interviewed by journalists looking for unique angles to make their column or their show come alive. My biography has been written and made into a motion picture. By this time, I should have been hit with every question imaginable about dealing with disability. Still, in the course of my twenty-year celebrity life, I can count on my fingers the number of times I was asked, "How did your blindness affect your parents? What did they feel? How did they handle it?"

Now to be very clear, I was often asked to talk to the interviewer about what my parents *did*, but not about what they *felt*. And so we come to the germinations that I hope will make this book interesting and informative.

We are about to go on a journey of parental hopes and dreams. Of heroism and disappointments. Of success and, yes, of failure, as we try to understand the complex emotions found inside the parents of children with disabilities.

Special Parent, Special Child is not a "how to raise a child with a disability" text. My design is to allow parents to speak openly, intimately, and in depth about their feelings and experiences without the formation of conclusions by professionals, who rarely have been the parents of children with disabilities themselves.

I chose this approach because after reviewing the literature on disability I found that almost all the works were written by people with disabilities. When they spoke of their parents' participation, it was from their point of view, rather than from specific parent interviews. Until now, I had not thought about how my life had affected my mother and father, probably because I was a disabled person. It was *my* handicap, *my* cross to bear. One of the issues facing people with disabilities all through their lives is their own selfishness. Or maybe I ought to say, their own "self-centeredness." The disability is so demanding, so totally consuming, that the disabled person very often loses perspective or empathy for others.

This book serves as a work that lets the parents' voices be heard. The wonderful conversation with my mother was not the only reason to write this book. I also believe that the future of people with disabilities has come to a crossroad in American society. With the passage of the Americans With Disabilities Act and the implementation of the Child's Rights Act that became law in the mid-eighties, words like "advocacy" and "inclusion," formerly buzzwords, are now being implemented as part of our system of education.

I want to make it clear that I am an advocate of the philosophy of total inclusion. However, as our parent stories will point out, the road to inclusion for children with disabilities is fraught with potholes and parental anguish. A law, or the passage of an act, has nothing to do with operational realities. And that is where we find ourselves when viewing the state of education for children with disabilities.

To grasp the perspective, we need to once again look back to my mother. When I was born, it was felt that blind children should be educated in schools specifically for the blind. I grew up in Massachusetts and attended the Perkins School for the Blind in Watertown, Mass. During that period, Perkins was thought of as the premier program for the education of all blind children. Yet the students were totally isolated from daily participation with sighted children. This philosophy of isolation education was the posture of almost every group that related to children with disabilities. Schools for the deaf, schools for the retarded, and specialized programs for wheelchair-bound kids dominated our educational approach to children with disability. Consequently, parents became focused only on the issues that pertained directly to their child. My mother, for example, belonged to a national organization of parents of blind children.

Though I'm sure she would have been sensitive to the special needs of children with different disabilities, she was totally absorbed by her blind son and his specific needs.

Today the philosophy of inclusion, and of placing children in the least-restrictive environment compels parents to take a new look at the common ground they share with other parents who have children with varying disabilities. This book attempts to frame that common ground not by dictating a message to the parents who are being interviewed but by allowing them to take us on their personal journeys and then comparing the information gathered.

This work is truly nonscientific. There is no effort to be statistical or to compel the reader to believe its conclusions are etched in stone. However, in preparing to write this work, I spoke to over two-hundred families and picked the six that I felt could express the totality of the problem with the most insight and eloquence.

GUIDEPOSTS

In attempting to chart the common ground that parents with disabled children share, I am going to present a road map of issues to look for as the parents' stories move us through these pages.

Initial Reaction to Professionals

First there seems to be a general mistrust on the part of the parents when they discuss the way in which they were treated by health care professionals during the birth of their children. Given the overriding concerns of the public about medical malpractice, it may be that this is not a particularly notable trend. But the parents of children with disabilities certainly react strongly when discussing the total treatment and the bedside manners of their doctors.

Denial

Then there is the recognition of the disability and the parental denial of that disability. My mother noted earlier that she hung onto every possible hope when one of the ophthalmologists my parents consulted told her that I would have, at minimum, light perception. Following that special talk we had on her eightieth birthday, she subsequently told me that she did not accept blindness as a part of her reality for at least four months after my diagnosis. I believe that every parent must go through denial if there is ever to be growth. I have known some parents with children of disability who seem so positive, I always felt that some day they would crack emotionally. As history has recorded, heroes that rise from the ashes of human misfortune can become even more successful. Parent heroes rise from denial to be truly noble advocates on behalf of their children with disabilities.

Grieving

Along with denial comes the grieving or mourning period. Parents talk about not having the perfect child. My mother totally denied this concept, deciding early to make her child perfect. Frankly, she failed horribly, but I am grateful for all of her efforts. In the face of this loss, parents feel desperate to compensate. They do that by going on what I call the "parent search." They read everything they can get their hands on relating to the disability, and often read everything they can find on any disability they think might touch their lives. They also tend to pursue every scheme possible in order to find quick solutions for their child. It is only when they accept the idea that he or she will be a child with special needs that they begin to be able to move forward as loving advocates.

Family Repercussions

For all of the parents of Special-Needs children, this is a wrenching time. Often they attach blame to themselves for their child's disability. Many marriages get stretched to the breaking point and, frankly, statistics show that many don't survive. Relations with extended family members can become distant because the parents are so absorbed, they believe no extended family member could ever understand their problems. And then there are the siblings. In many cases, siblings suffer grave consequences because parents are forced into an all-consuming involvement with the Special-Needs child.

Working the System

Parents next face accessing the system of therapeutic and educational possibilities available for their child. This is a period of starts and stops in the road. There can be tremendous disappointment as parents wrestle with the system, trying to sort out appropriate choices. Eventually, this process of rehab or therapy, or early tutoring intervention, leads to the question of education, and here the parent dilemma becomes highly charged. If inclusion is effectively utilized, the child with a disability will, under the law, receive an education in the least-restrictive environment, but that education is also required to support his or her special needs. In order to achieve this goal, the parents participate in the development of an appropriate Individual Education Plan (IEP) relating to their child. Theoretically, all the people who will touch the education and socialization of the child with special needs will participate in the IEP, and realistic goals will be set and developed. In practice, the IEP is a parental nightmare, because unless the parents are aggressive advocates, willing to take the special issues of their children all the way to the wall, most IEP meetings last fifteen minutes and produce hasty conclusions.

Advocacy

So we come to the moment when parents must aggressively get into the game. Children with disabilities can fall through the cracks and get categorized right from the first IEP. For example, a child with a learning disability may be defined as mentally handicapped, rather than simply learning disabled. If an inappropriate track is chosen at the beginning, it is virtually impossible for the child, ever, to climb out of the bureaucratic box he or she is placed in. Parents must come to this fundamental truth: *they understand their child better than anyone else,* and their instinct must dominate the appropriate education given to that special child. Professionals provide access, knowledge, and tools that can carry the child to a happy educational conclusion. But parents are both the advocates and the weather vanes defining the growth track that their children should be on.

Loss of Identity

The process of raising a child with a disability is so complex that parents can lose their sense of self-worth. They become so absorbed in the special needs of their loved one that they see themselves only as the parent of a child with a disability, rather than as a whole human being who has the right to an extended and fulfilling life. Throughout my public life, I have received hundreds of letters from parents who always refer to themselves as the parent of a child with a disability. In these letters, I never seem to learn anything else about the parent. And when attending parent conferences on disability, the intensity is extraordinary, and the commitment that I sense is absolute. I am not suggesting that parents should not be completely involved with their children. I am pointing out that in order for them to truly serve the needs of those children with disabilities, they must be able to have an appropriate sense of humor and an understanding that the battles they fight are not won every day. These skirmishes are simply endless, and need to be thought of as an ongoing part of life.

The Socialization Process

How do parents integrate their child with disabilities into a standard children's peer group set? The issue is very complicated, because it connects not only to the environment the child was raised in but to the special issues he or she must confront. In my case, my parents began my life by isolating me. The theory was to put a fence around my backyard so that I would not get hurt. My play was inside the fence, with the world outside. It wasn't until fortune smiled, and a wonderful little boy named Billy Hannon moved in next door, that my life changed. I also was fortunate because I was blessed with unique musical, academic, and athletic talents that provided me with access to a wonderful life. But disabilities that include developmental delays may substantially complicate the possibility of standard social interaction with peer groups.

Ongoing Relationship with Professionals

The parent relationship with the professionals who touch the lives of their children with special needs can only be described as complex at best. Generally, parents see the professional as someone who is not doing enough on behalf of their child, and the professional sees the parent as someone who generally doesn't understand the tensions that go with the profession, be it teaching, counseling, therapy, medicine, or school administration. It is my hope that these critical communications will improve on behalf of children with disabilities. The system cannot grow without mutual respect and trust, and that trust can only develop through open dialogue and increased understanding.

Strength and Hope

When reading this chapter, it would be easy to believe that the lives of parents with Special-Needs children are based on gloom and doom. That is not true. Parents constantly talk about the life lessons they've learned from their children. They believe they are better people because of the circumstances they have confronted, and they talk about reservoirs of strength they did not know they possessed. The interaction of parents with their Special-Needs children and our society in general can only be described as challenging. And now that we have engaged ourselves in the process of inclusion, we must search for the common purpose that brings us together.

Parents must build bridges that help children with disabilities gain true inclusion. Learning to create appropriate dialogue with professionals and coming to understand how to access the supports that exist in the system clearly are the biggest jobs for the parent of a child with special needs. In the stories that you will read dealing with the ongoing struggle of our special parents, I believe that you will come to understand how these people learned to access the system. Also I think you'll find that the system can only be moved forward when parents learn to understand the common ground they share. If the system of inclusion and least-restrictive environment is going to work, the people most involved, that is, the parents, need to come together collectively to act as a powerful lobby for growth and change serving the children they all love.

When I began this project, I believed I had a solid understanding about the issues relating to children with disabilities. I found out I knew absolutely nothing. I only knew how to be a person with a disability, and, in retrospect, I only knew that because of the loving training gained from my mother and my father, along with appropriate supports, both academically and emotionally, provided by professionals.

So now you will begin this journey into the lives of parents with Special-Needs children. If you are the parent of a child with a disability, I hope you will see the common thread that ties all of you together. If you are a professional, I hope this will give you cause for thought about how you deal with these vulnerable families. And if you are a person with a disability, I hope you will read these pages as I lived this experience, with a feeling of gratitude for all of the commitment demonstrated by these special people.

Lindy and Nick

I HAVE KNOWN LINDY SOUZA ALLEN since she was a little girl. We met in the summer of 1966, in Lindy's home, on Cape Cod. Her brother Phil and I were roommates at Providence College, and we used to come to the Cape to enjoy the most wonderful summer experiences any college kid could ever hope for. There's no place more beautiful than Cape Cod, and there has never been a family like the Souzas.

Jim and Betty became everybody's mom and dad, opening their home and their hearts to all of Phil's college friends, but especially to Tom Sullivan and later, to Patty and our children. When I married Patty and got my first job playing piano on Cape Cod, Jim and Betty rented us one of the cottages on their property and were involved in the early raising of our children, Blythe and Tom. Through all those years, I had the chance to watch Lindy grow up. She was a part of our family. She baby-sat for our children, sailed with me, and loved sharing special little girl things with Patty.

I like to think that a part of Lindy's sensitivity toward disability stems from those early years on Cape Cod with us. But if I'm really honest, I have to say that Lindy Souza is Lindy Souza. She is simply special, and she became more special when she fell in love with my friend Nick Allen, the best dad I ever met.

Nick came from a somewhat different family background. Though his family loved him, his mom and dad were separated early, and Nick talks often of, in his words, "raising himself." That made him self-reliant, and I suppose probably also made him able to cope with what would come later as he and Lindy raised their little boy, Sean.

Sometimes the pieces of the puzzle of life seem fated, and I suppose that is the case in the Allen family. Nick and Lindy have not just been the parents of a child with a disability. They have celebrated the uniqueness of that child, defining the commitment that every human being ought to feel toward his or her family. That is not to say that the road has been easy. I was shaken as we examined their lives, and the life of their son, Sean, throughout their interview.

Our conversation took place on Nantucket, the beautiful island off the east coast of Cape Cod. I had come there to give a speech. Nick and Lindy took the ferry over from Falmouth to Nantucket, and we sat in a beautiful rented cottage, on three incredible July days, sharing emotion and information. Because I've known Lindy since she was a little girl, I could tell from the beginning that she was stressed. It was only at the end of that first day, while we were having dinner and drinks, that she explained she had found it difficult to go back into the past and talk about the pain they had experienced.

I used to believe that it was impossible to remember past sickness or pain in vivid terms, but I could hear Lindy's physical discomfort as she related stories about their early experiences with Sean. As he always does, Nick took on the role of support and quiet strength. I suppose he could see on Lindy's face that the interview created tension and discomfort. Having realized this might be a problem, I began by asking them an easy question: "How did you meet and what impressions did you have of each other?"

Lindy laughed. "Oh, we met in a bar just like you and Patty did."

"Funny," I said, "how those bar relationships work out. But what qualities did you find in Nick that drew you to him?"

She paused. "I could tell he was a good guy, right from the beginning."

"And you, Nick, what kind of feelings did you get from Lindy?"

He didn't hesitate. "She was honest," he said. "She told you like it really was. I like that a lot. It's easy to tell where you stand that way."

"Nick, what were you doing at that time? Were you in school or working?"

"I was working two jobs, and taking as many classes as I could."

Lindy interrupted. "I suppose that's what I loved about him so much. He was already building a house, while he was working and going to school. I knew that this guy was on top of it, that he could take care of himself, and I suppose, take care of me."

Those were pretty practical reasons to get married. But over the years, I've realized how in love these two people really are. I leaned back in my chair. "I'd like to approach our work in three distinct areas. First, let's talk about everything that relates to the physical part of your life with Sean. Then we'll tackle the question of socialization and finally education. Lindy, how long after you were married did you get pregnant?"

"Well, we got married in 1980. I got pregnant with Sean in 1983, at the same time that my sister, Connie, did. She had a great deal of difficulty becoming pregnant. When we were both going through this, I remember my mother expressing her disappointment that I was pregnant while Nick was still in school. Maybe there was some mother's wisdom in her feelings."

"So other than your mother's feelings," I said, "was Sean a fairly normal pregnancy?"

"He was a very normal pregnancy. I felt great. I was managing a clothing store at that time, and I had gone for one of my appointments. I was thirty-two and a half weeks along. I was experiencing some bleeding, and so I figured I'd better talk to the doctor about it. But he said, 'You're just getting bigger; that's normal.' Sean was born three days later. Nick and I went to the Barnstable County Fair with mom and dad. And I said, 'You know, I really feel awful.'

"Mom must have been a mindreader because she said, 'Well, wouldn't it be funny if you had the baby now, even though it's early.' Anyway, I feel that if the doctor had done a thorough check, he would have noticed that I was dilated. Saturday morning I woke up already in labor. It was my last day of work, and I was committed to doing the job."

Nick jumped in. "I wasn't about to let her go to work. She's stubborn. I knew it might have been false labor, but I was going to make her go to the hospital anyway. I called the doctor. He was real casual. 'Yes,' he said, 'bring her in.' But then things started going real fast."

"When we arrived at the hospital, I was already eight centimeters dilated," Lindy said. "The doctor told us that he would love it if they could fly me to Boston, but he felt that it was too late, and he was right. I mean, one push and Sean was here. The birth took only forty-five minutes."

Nick said, "You know, I guess we were lucky. The doctor who delivered Sean wasn't actually our obstetrician."

"You mean you had a different doctor?"

"Yes," Nick said, "and it was good that we did. I mean, our own doctor missed the diagnosis. We never did anything about it, but the fact is, Lindy came into the hospital bleeding, probably dilated, and look what happened. Sean was born and this guy missed it."

"Do you hold the doctor accountable, Nick?"

"Not really. Well, maybe I do, but it's water under the bridge now."

"Were you present through the labor and delivery?"

"I was and it was scary. That's the only word I can use to describe it, scary. Everything was happening so fast around us. People were trying to be calm, but I could feel their tension. This wasn't a celebration, like you hear about in the movies, this was serious stuff, and we weren't prepared for it."

"We sure weren't," Lindy added. "We hadn't even gone through Lamaze. I was so busy working, I figured we would get to that. We intended to start class the next week. Sean was born at seven and a half months, I figured there was still plenty of time."

Nick laughed. "So forty-five minutes later Sean was here. He was a perfect-looking baby. They ran the Apgar test on him, and everything seemed normal."

"What's the Apgar test?" I asked.

"It's a series of immediate-reaction tests the doctors give infants to see if everything's okay."

"And with Sean, everything was?" I asked.

"It seemed to be, at least that's what the doctor said."

"Lindy, did you feel any sense of misgiving, or concern about Sean?"

"Oh, sure I did, Tom. First of all, they took him away from

me right away. And even though he seemed to be breathing okay, everything was happening too fast all around us. Maybe it's that mother's instinct again, but I knew something was wrong."

Nick said, "They put him in an incubator in the nursery and kept him away from other children. They had oxygen and other lines hooked up to him, and a nurse with him all the time. You know, Cape Cod Hospital just isn't equipped to handle complex cases, and so I was already getting worried. He stayed hooked up there for a couple of hours, and then they brought him to Lindy."

Lindy turned to him. "Do you remember how we were laughing because Sean was making those grunting noises? Only later we found out that meant he had the beginnings of a breathing problem."

"So what did they tell you?" I asked.

Nick said, "They told us that Sean had not produced surfactant, a natural lubricant for the lungs that we all need to breathe effectively. They were calling the Massachusetts General Hospital Neo-Natal Unit. An ambulance was on its way with a team to take Sean to Boston."

"Oh my God," I said. "I can't even imagine how you felt."

"I don't know if we were able to feel anything," Lindy replied. "We were still in shock. I remember one thing for sure. They brought Sean to me just before they put him in the ambulance, and do you know that little boy took hold of my finger. He actually held on to my finger. It made me feel so much like his mother, and then he was gone.

"Then a woman who just had a baby was brought into my room. She was sharing the room with me. And she had a normal, healthy baby, and I broke down. Nick told the hospital staff that they had to get me a room by myself. It's funny though, even at her worst, a mother still can do some amazing things. I told the nurses I wanted to start pumping milk for

Sean. They didn't suggest it; nobody suggested it. I just knew he needed it. Maybe parents are advocates for their children right from the beginning. It seems that way now when I look back."

Nick leaned forward in his chair. "The staff was awful. They gave me a hard time about moving Lindy to another room. I was young, I probably didn't fight hard enough. Lindy, do you remember the nurse that talked to us?"

"I'll never forget her," she said. "When she walked into my room, and I was crying, she said to me, 'Melinda, your baby will be just fine.' I can't ever get her out of my head."

"So they took Sean away to Boston. How long was he there?"

"For twelve days," Nick said.

"And what did you do during that time?"

"We called, we visited, we worried, and we prayed," Nick remembered. "We'd see him in the Neo-Natal Unit and he looked good. He didn't have the birth marks that come when babies are full-term. He actually looked good because he was premature."

"I wonder if that was a protection even then, your way of avoiding what you were afraid might be the realities."

"Oh, I'm not that smart, Tom, but I think I felt he looked good because I wanted to believe everything would be okay."

"So twelve days go by, and you're going to bring him home?"

"That's right, we were going to bring him home," Nick said. "A resident even asked us if we had a carseat with us so that Sean would be okay while we were driving."

"You mean, when you took Sean home, you believed that everything was normal?"

"We did. We thought that if we brought him home and got some weight on him, everything would be okay. We believed that the worst was behind us, and that we could take care of whatever else happened. We were actually excited about being new parents."

Lindy laughed. "The bottles were like little doll bottles, and the diapers, they were so small."

Nick went on. "But we were coping. I was even going to school and taking exams during the week we brought him home. We just didn't think anything was wrong."

"So what started you wondering?" I asked.

Lindy put her hand on her chin. "Sean was an irritable baby. It's hard to understand that because now he's so terrific. But back then, we couldn't take him anywhere. He fussed all the time. I feel badly because I probably overreacted in many situations by isolating him and being overprotective. For all I know, he was in a lot of pain. I just didn't understand. Everybody categorized him as an irritable baby. I don't think my family liked him very much, and frankly I can't blame them."

Nick said, "We couldn't take him into a restaurant. We had to eat separately; one of us had to be outside with him while the other was finishing dinner."

"Was that because Sean became overstimulated?" I asked. "We talked about stimulation when you visited me last year."

"Tom, you were the first person to bring this up," Lindy replied. "You thought it was related to how the brain sends electronic impulses through the nervous system."

"Oh, Lindy," I said, "I'm not a medical expert. This is just the opinion of an amateur."

"But you're right, Tom," Lindy said. "From the time Sean was a baby, certain situations seemed to overstimulate him, and caused him to have a reaction."

"Sounds can make him crazy," Nick said. "And there are things that he just doesn't like to touch. Sometimes he finds it really difficult to be in large crowds, like at sports events. I don't believe that he's afraid, it's just that every nerve ending must be vibrating. He must build up levels of conditioned stress."

"I think it's like my reaction when chalk rubs across a blackboard, or someone is cutting meat and scrapes the knife on the plate. That feels awful. The sound goes right up my spine and makes my face vibrate! I hate it."

We all laughed. I went on.

"So I'm sure some high-priced neurologist could develop a test procedure to find out how many different things disturb Sean this way. We'd probably all be surprised at the size of the list."

Lindy nodded. "Isn't it amazing that after being Sean's parents all these years, there's still so much about his disability we don't understand. It's like the old saying; you can't know a person until you've walked in his moccasins. None of us will ever know how much Sean has been affected, right from birth, by things that we could not possibly comprehend.

"It was the worst at holidays. I'll never forget Thanksgiving and Christmas when our relatives brought their children. It was awful. Sean was just inconsolable. He'd cry and I'd cry. Probably everybody was crying. My mother said he was just a colicky baby. I must have agreed, because everything else seemed okay. He was gaining weight. The only thing I noticed was that he was always throwing up when he burped."

"Lindy, I don't know if that seems so unusual. You were a first-time mom, and Nick, you were a first-time dad. You couldn't have had all the answers. So the months went by and you didn't sense anything unusual? What about the doctors, do you think they should have known more? Should they have had a better sense that something different was going on?"

Lindy laughed, a little sarcastically. "Well, we took Sean to Massachusetts General for constant checkups. At two months, at four months, at six months. Nobody noticed anything. The neurologist hid behind the idea that Sean was developmentally delayed. That's an interesting phrase. It lets you obscure a lot of problems. And then at nine months we went to the head of neurology at Massachusetts General. He looked at Sean's entire body under a powerful light, examining the blood vessels, and then he said, 'Your boy is doing just fine.' A resident noticed some spasticity in Sean's legs, but the doctor was quick to say, 'Oh no, he's fine.' And we took him home again."

"So when did you finally understand that something was really wrong with your son?"

"It's amazing, Tom. I guess it always comes down to parents having the right instincts. I'd gone over to my sister Connie's house, for a visit. Her little boy and Sean are about the same age. She invited a friend named Karen, who also had a son, Sean, about the same age. Ryan and Karen's Sean went through the day just fine. And my son cried non-stop. It was awful. Karen said, 'You know, Lindy, I really think you should have Sean evaluated.' She suggested that I take him to an Early Intervention Program on Cape Cod designed to examine his early development."

"And what happened?" I asked.

"Well, they evaluated him, and came out to me and said, 'Your son is much, much too delayed. We suggest you get a second opinion.' It's astounding how terrific Early Intervention is. It's a whole team of people who operate on behalf of your child. There's physical therapists, educators, occupational therapists, all of them a part of the team. And they were sure that something was profoundly wrong."

"And there was no doctor on the team?" I asked.

"No. In fact, when they filed their report, they all talked about how remarkable it was that Sean had done even as well as he had. They credited it to the way Nick and I interacted with him, that we would hold him and sing to him, and be totally interactive in his early life."

"But nobody's used the words *cerebral palsy*?"

Lindy said, "That didn't happen until we saw a young doctor who'd just come to the town of Orleans. I read about her in the newspaper because she was involved with early developmentally delayed children. She was the first person to tell me that Sean had cerebral palsy. But even then it didn't actually sink in. That only happened when we went to a neurologist in Hyannis, a couple of months later. He confirmed that Sean had cerebral palsy, and he told me to just take him home and love him. No directed approach, no sense of what we ought to do. Just take him home and love him."

I could hear a tear in Lindy's voice when she said that. Then she went on.

"And we got letters from people that sounded like condolences after we told them that Sean had cerebral palsy. It was as if there'd been a death in the family, and I suppose we went through a grieving process. Picture it, Tom. A doctor takes you into the office and sits you down, and tells you your child has cerebral palsy. He doesn't actually define what that is—just damage to the motor parts of the brain—and in Sean's case, he figures it is probably mostly from the waist down. He can't tell us how delayed Sean would be.

"Probably all parents of children with disabilities have to go through this grieving process. I don't think anybody can understand it unless they've experienced it. Most doctors have no 'people skills.' Maybe they've seen too many patients, maybe they're anesthetized to the trauma they create in people's lives by telling them the truth, but they certainly don't win the sensitivity award.

"And it's hard to believe that all of this happened when Sean was a year old. It took one year of his life before anyone identified his cerebral palsy. Either we were really insensitive, or the system wasn't working. All of us have to do a lot better at recognizing the issues early."

"Nick, up to this point you were going to school, you were working, you just built a house in Brewster. You were busy full-time. Were you involved in this part of Sean's life?"

"I think so, Tom. But I have to say that the pressure is much more on the mother than it is on the dad."

Lindy interrupted. "I think that's true, but, Nick, you were always a great father. Sean used to like to play in the backyard pool with you, and I remember how you'd hold him at night."

"Thanks for saying that, dear." Nick laughed. "But the truth is, mothers do an awful lot more than dads."

I felt like I was listening to apologies. Lindy jumped in again. "Yes, but I think that's the nature of being a mother. This was my job, you had other jobs to do."

"Lindy, how did you tell the rest of your family about Sean's CP?"

"Actually I didn't. Early Intervention suggested a meeting for all the family members. The Early Intervention people explained that Sean was not the baby everybody expected him to be. He had cerebral palsy. It was a real stressful meeting. I don't think it had to be like that."

"But, Lindy," I said, "you know, those folks are in the business of crisis management. They have to intervene that way."

She thought about that and then went on almost as if she were thinking out loud. "Yes, but I don't think that I really enjoyed the first year of my baby's life. I was so involved in his care, I just, well . . . I just didn't really get involved in the joy of having him. Of being his mother."

I tried to sum up. "Let me see if I've got everything right. Sean is a year old. You've understood that he has cerebral palsy, that his problems are perceived as generally from the waist down, but you don't know how his speech and language will develop."

Lindy interrupted. "The professionals even recommended that I start teaching him sign language. We never did that. I was committed to the idea that he would talk."

I laughed. "And he sure does talk. So you know that it's going to be a long road, but he seemed somewhat stable at this point, right?"

Nick said, "Perspective really is a big part of this. When you can't diagnose a CP child until he's about a year old, it usually means that the child isn't going to be as delayed. So I guess we were doing better than a lot of people. And then they told us that Sean was probably going to have seizures."

"Oh my God," I said. "Seizures on top of everything else? Lindy, who was talking to you now? Were you getting these diagnoses from doctors or what?"

"All this information was coming from the Early Intervention people. I owe so much to a woman named Cindy Fox. She was our family coordinator, and she did an incredible job. She kept our lives together. But it still comes down to parenting skills. They were trying to help us. We even had to tape Sean's sounds to prove to them that he could speak. And I did all kinds of things to keep exercising his muscles, trying to help control the spasticity. If Early Intervention has a problem, it's that they treat so many different disabilities, it's easy for them to generalize. But parents still have to be totally involved in figuring out their child's specific needs."

"That's true," I said. "When I was a little boy, and there was no Early Intervention and no support services to help, my mother had to decide what I could and couldn't do, and she charted the course of my growing up as a blind child. I bet if I asked her today, she'd say that she made some mistakes, but for the most part, her instincts were a lot better than any of the professionals who were just beginning to learn about blindness."

"Tom, we didn't always make the right decisions," Nick added. "I remember when Sean was about a year old, he had to go for a CAT scan. We took him to Cape Cod Hospital. We

were supposed to give him a tablespoon of hydrochlorine before he went for the CAT scan to relax him so that we could get
him into the machine. Well, we got there and the machine was
broken, and he'd had one tablespoon. The technician said, 'Give
him another one.' I did, and boy was it scary. Sean became
totally flaccid, his muscles wouldn't work. He was absolutely
drugged out. It was a horrible thing for us to do, but we believed
in the professionals. That taught us a valuable lesson. You can't
ask too many questions. As a parent, you have to satisfy yourself that the doctors and the technicians are doing the right
thing for your son. We've lived by that rule ever since."

Lindy took Nick's hand. "I'm so glad Nick is the way he is.
That day there was a radiologist at the hospital. What did he
know about our son? He just took X rays. He told us not to
worry about this reaction. It's a lot like someone who's drunk.
'Just take him home,' he said, 'he'll be okay.' So we did. And for
the next eight hours Sean didn't even move; he was totally out. I
couldn't face it. I sat downstairs and kept yelling up to Nick, 'Is
everything all right? Is he all right?' Nick sat with Sean all
night."

"Do you two think that this is an important part of parenting? Sometimes one parent can deal with problems, and the
other one can't?"

"There's no question about it," Nick said. "I seemed to be
good during Sean's physical crises. I know a lot about the
mechanics of his CP, and how to help him when he's dealing
with those problems. But Lindy is great at confronting professionals: dealing with doctors and educators. I tend to have too
much respect for their professionalism. So I guess you're right,
Tom, parents do pick up the slack for each other. If a family is
working, I suppose we all fill in the spaces." He laughed. "Yes,
but sometimes we don't get the spaces all filled in. When Sean
was five or six months old, we noticed that his eyes were
crossing. We took him to an ophthalmologist and found out he

had strabismus. The guy recommended that Sean have surgery right away."

"For strabismus?" I asked. "Wasn't that the least of his problems?"

"That's right," Nick said. "But we had the surgery anyway. At this point, Sean had ophthalmologists, occupational therapists, physical therapists, and neurologists involved. Pretty soon we were going to have orthopedists and a pediatrician. All of these people were involved, but nobody took charge of the total management of Sean's health care."

Lindy laughed. "In most states, if we were indigent parents, we could get a case manager—somebody to come in and be the gatekeeper. But if you're doing well financially, it's almost impossible to get an overall approach from state support for the management of your child's issues. Parents have to become crisis managers, or maybe I ought to say case managers."

I took a deep breath. "Okay, let me go forward now with Sean's physical condition, and how you had to handle it. He has had surgery on his eyes, which to you seems out of context. Now, he's between fifteen and eighteen months old and going for a constant battery of tests."

"And those tests weren't fun," Nick said. "Even now when Sean takes X rays, he's afraid the camera is going to fall on him. That's because when he first went to Children's Hospital in Boston, the techs used to put sandbags on his arms and sometimes even around his legs, to keep him still for the X-ray machine. I've learned over the years to hold him myself. That keeps him a little more relaxed." There was a pause while all of us absorbed that painful idea.

"But at this point," I went on, "nobody has done anything yet about the CP. There's been no surgery related to it."

"Not yet," Nick said. "Sean was two years old before Dr. Kasser did the first surgery to release the muscles on the inside of his leg. These are the adductor muscles. When you picked Sean up, his legs would cross. By releasing the adductor muscles, the abductor muscles (in the outer thigh) compensated, keeping his legs apart. The doctors expected that when the legs came apart, the hip would go back into its socket."

"You mean, it was dislocated?"

"Yes, that's how the doctors explained it," Nick said. "But the surgery wasn't the only thing we had to do. Sean had to wear these crazy braces, to keep his legs apart. It used to take a half hour to put them on every night, and we couldn't get him comfortable on his stomach. And then there were the nerve blocks. They tried those, too. That's where they injected alcohol into the nerves to release some of the spasticity in his body. The whole thing was overwhelming."

"And did the surgery work?" I asked.

"Not really," Nick said. "Actually it was a disaster. After Sean had the surgery to get his legs apart, the doctors put him in a full body cast that ran from just under his armpits all the way to his feet. And then there was a bar between his legs, to keep his legs apart, to insure that when the muscles grew back, they would be lengthened."

"How long was Sean supposed to be in the bodycast?"

"For six weeks," Nick said. "But it didn't really work out very well. He started to get some swelling in his groin and penis, which was abnormal. We finally got a urologist to look at him. He said, 'Isn't there some way we can get this body cast off him?' And finally Dr. Kasser and the urologist talked and they took the body cast off. You know, within just a couple of hours the swelling went down. It amazes me that fate got these two doctors together because they might not have even communicated under ordinary circumstances. They just passed each other in the hall, and then they fixed Sean because they had a conversation together."

"I can't even imagine what it was like to have Sean in a body cast."

Nick said, "It was awful. And some things happened that really frightened us; sometimes it's impossible to handle a child the right way. When we lived in Brewster, we had wall heaters. One night a pillow that was resting against one began to smolder. We were asleep at the time and the smoke alarm woke us up. Actually I can't say that there was any danger of fire, but there sure was a lot of smoke and it frightened Sean to death. Also, Sean slept downstairs and when he woke up in the middle of the night, like all kids do, he had to urinate. He did it in his cast. It was a horrible situation."

"You probably blamed yourself," I said.

"Sure we did," Lindy said. "Parents are always doing that, especially when they have a child with a disability. You're just trying to cope with the complexity of the situation. When Sean urinated in his cast, we used a hair dryer to dry the inside. But then we became concerned about burning him. And I remember there was the time he was eating, and some food went down the wrong way. I couldn't clear the food from his esophagus easily when he was in a body cast, because I couldn't hold him upside down and bang him on the back. It was just too complicated. The whole thing is too complicated." We all became quiet. I had to go on.

"How many surgeries has Sean endured?"

Nick laughed. "A lot, and there are probably more to come. Well, let's see. There was the surgery for strabismus on his eyes, then the first surgery that Doctor Kasser did. Then there were the nerve blocks. And then there was the big surgery that Doctor Goldberg did a couple of summers ago. That was when they had Sean in a full body cast all over again."

"What was Doctor Goldberg trying to achieve in this operation?"

"The surgery is called a Stahali shelf," Nick explained. "The doctors take a piece of bone from the top of the hip, and put it over the socket, creating a new part of the socket that was dislocated. Then it's all held together by tendons and muscles. And while all this was being done, the doctors decided to do a whole lot of other muscle work."

"Could you see results right away?"

"Not really," Lindy said. "The surgery took eight hours and the recovery about a year."

"So after all this, do you feel like you can see the light at the end of the physical tunnel?"

"It's impossible to tell," Lindy went on. "With Sean's spastic cerebral palsy, you just never know."

"How did you pay for all this?"

Nick laughed again. "Well, thank goodness we live in the state of Massachusetts. It's a very progressive state. I've got Blue Cross/Blue Shield. But there's a high deductible, and that's made up for by another state-run program which allows me to purchase supplementary coverage for about fifty dollars a month. Parents really have to learn about this. It's all part of taking care of a child with a disability."

"So while we're on costs, I can't even estimate what you must have spent for equipment."

Nick spoke up again. "It's not just what you spend, Tom, it's how long it takes to get what you need. By the time you fill out all the forms, and go through the state procedures to get a wheelchair, six months can go by. And every time you present Sean with a new piece of equipment, it's a psychological trauma. Not only does he have to learn to use it, but he also has to learn to accept it. And we have to figure out how to understand it. I'll tell you though, we just got him the first fun piece of equipment he's ever had. It's an adaptive bike. He just loves to ride it."

Lindy interrupted with a laugh, and this time it was a happy one. "Yes, but that cost five hundred dollars. It was money wonderfully spent. But you know, you'd better keep our accounting business going. Find more clients that have to pay those extended taxes."

Now they were both laughing.

"Have we covered everything relating to Sean's physical evolution?"

"I think so," Nick said. "But I'd like to say it's the intensity of every day that I want parents to understand. From the time Sean gets up in the morning to the time he goes to bed at night, we have to project how he can achieve some level of normalcy."

Lindy picked up. "It's never really normal. But the state of normalcy is what we're talking about. We're always finding ways for Sean to interact even with his physical disability. Parents with physically challenged children not only are the caregivers, they also have to be their own case managers, crisis intervention specialists, and even diagnosticians as they try to sort out all the medical opinions. They have to understand the processes of physical therapy, and they have to be technicians when it comes to understanding the adaptive equipment. Parents have to be willing to follow their instincts, and support those instincts with as much knowledge as they can gain on behalf of their child."

"Okay," I said, "that's enough for day one. Let's get some dinner. We could all use a drink, and watch the sunset on this beautiful island. We'll tackle the rest tomorrow."

After a great night's sleep with the ocean air coming through our open windows, we got together the next morning. I noticed immediately that Lindy and Nick were much more relaxed; we were going to talk about sociological and educational issues.

Lindy began. "Medicine and mechanics just seem overwhelming to me. When we talk about Sean's psychological adjustment, and his education, these are things I can get my hands around, that I can understand. I guess maybe they're easier to cope with. I feel like I can do more to solve the problems."

"Well, let's start then with the education of a child with CP."

"Tom, we were so lucky to be living in the state of Massachusetts because under state law every child has to be offered educational opportunities until they're twenty-two. And because I had found Early Intervention, Sean really began his educational process early. When he graduated from Early Intervention at three, I had a pretty good understanding of what was available. But what's available and what works—those are two different things."

"Nick, were professionals using buzzwords then, like 'inclusion' and 'mainstreaming'?"

"I'd heard the word mainstreaming, but inclusion wasn't happening yet. Sean was going to become part of special-class situations."

"You know, folks, I've always felt that isolates disabled children even more. We put them in a normal school setting but then set them apart in special classrooms so they have no interaction with normal children."

"I agree," Nick said. "At least it's getting better now."

Lindy went on. "I want you to understand, Tom, that we were trying to bridge the gap early. Sean was going to a preschool Special-Needs class, but I also had him enrolled in a normal preschool to try and, I'll use their word now, 'to include him.' I'll never forget how I felt when Sean would go off in the morning to preschool. I don't think I was much good for anyone that year, I was so worried about how he was doing. Plus, I was broken-hearted. I put him on the special school bus provided for Special-Needs children every morning. I just shattered inside letting him go that way, and he was inconsolable. It's so wrenching for 'Special-Needs' parents."

"I remember that," I said. "When I was a little boy, my parents sent me to boarding school. Every Sunday night they used to have to take me back to Perkins—that was the Blind School—and I'd kick and scream and my mother or my sisters would cry. My father would say, 'Oh, the hell with school. We don't have to send him anywhere. We'll educate him ourselves.'"

"Tom, there were times when I thought about keeping Sean home and doing just that. This has to be one of the toughest moments in the life of a Special-Needs family. But I have to stop here and note Cindy Fox's contribution again. She had left Early Intervention and become one of Sean's preschool teachers. She really understood the need for inclusion. She was very much ahead of her time."

"I'm glad you brought that up, Lindy. It seems to me that sometimes people get the impression that parents do things all by themselves, that they're advocates all alone. I guess you really can't be an advocate unless you have professionals who truly understand your advocacy. Are those people few and far between?" I asked.

"Not really," Nick said. "I've come to believe that all parents can get what they need if they understand how to use the system. The key is to figure out how. There are plenty of programs in the bureaucracy, the question is sorting it through."

"Lindy, I understand how difficult it was for you to send Sean off to school on his own. Did you get involved in the classroom?"

"I tried that, but it wasn't very successful. Because I was there, Sean became more isolated in the other kids' eyes. Now we have a formula for this whole process. I think parents have to aggressively approach educational inclusion, or even inclusion in the socialization process, and then they have to back off, and hope it works out. It's helpful if you have a faith. You pray a lot."

"What was it like in the morning, when you had to get Sean up and ready for school?"

"Sean was in diapers until he was five. Potty training was a real issue for him because he couldn't feel himself going. His cerebral palsy is called spastic diplegia, meaning the muscles are always in spasms. There are other forms of CP, but because of the spasms, I'm not sure how much Sean really felt below his waist. Since he was in diapers for so long, we would have to get him up in the morning, carry him downstairs, put him in a special chair, change his diapers, dress him, and then carry him out to the school bus. When he got to school, they used to pull him around on a little red wagon. It sounds worse than it was. I think Sean loved the wagon. But getting him ready for school was tough. There are so many extra hours of child care in the life of a parent with a Special-Needs child."

"Folks, as you put in these hours, are there things that you realized about Sean that the professionals missed?"

"Oh a lot of them," Lindy said. "First of all, there was what we call the "in and out" syndrome. Sometimes Sean seemed to turn his brain way up so he could absorb everything all around him, and then other times he just seemed to miss the things that, to us, would seem most obvious. It's an odd, quirky thing. Then there's this business of overstimulation. There are situations that he cannot handle. You remember when you came to visit us last summer, and he freaked out at the Fourth of July fireworks?"

"I do remember that, Lindy, but I remember most of all how well Nick handled him."

"Oh, I just tried to do the best I could," Nick said. "He freaks out at a lot of things like that. Even when you change the water from the tub to the shower, that drives him crazy. Sirens and loud noises bother him. It's just one of those odd things about kids with CP that professionals don't understand."

"You really have to know your own child," Lindy said. "You have to know how to push the buttons to get him to give a little extra, to try a little harder. I think a child with a disability has to try harder just to be equal."

"I agree with you, Lindy. And I think only parents understand that part of the equation. The hardest thing in the world is for a parent to find the balance between being objective enough to recognize the problem and work logically toward a solution, and subjective enough to understand the unique nature of their child and how to work with his special needs.

"But let's move on. After Sean had been involved in Early Intervention and in preschool, it came time to send him to kindergarten. What was that like?"

"First, you have to remember that Sean was still in diapers. So you can imagine what happened. The other kids saw his diapers, and they laughed. He was assigned a one-on-one assistant in kindergarten, who made it one of her goals to get Sean potty-trained. Even though I have a lot of mixed feelings about her in terms of what happened later, I do credit her with that."

"Was Sean's kindergarten class a Special-Needs class, or was he in a class of inclusion?"

"It was a class of inclusion, but the kindergarten teacher was a pretty young girl. Then again, we were pretty young parents. The summer before kindergarten started, she came over to our house to get to know Sean. The conversation was terrific. We talked about what Sean was interested in, and she seemed comfortable enough. But as the year progressed, it was quite obvious that she felt uncomfortable. Whatever Sean got out of kindergarten, he got from the classroom assistant."

"Can you give me an example?"

"We had a notebook that went back and forth to school. I started picking up the teacher's comments, such as, 'From now on, when it comes to papertime, Sean will be taken to the back of the room and he and I will work on the papers together.' I didn't send my kid to kindergarten for him to be excluded from the rest of the class. Kindergarten is an emotional experience, and should have been the start of friendships for him—and friendships for me, forming with parent groups. All of that should have been happening at the same time. Looking back, I really should have followed my gut feelings about this. But at that time, I didn't have one other person involved with Sean in the school who understood the circumstances that he had to face."

Nick interrupted, trying to be fair again. "Yes, but Sean was the first person the school had ever dealt with who had his kinds of problems."

Lindy was dynamic. "Look, I decided early that I had to get involved. I wish today that I'd gotten even more involved. It drove me crazy that Sean wasn't going out for recess. They kept him working on the papers he hadn't finished. So we brought that up to the powers that be. I even started calling parents of the normies in the class to ask them what they thought, and they did step in to help me. The parents acknowledged that their kids were told to stay away from Sean. Imagine that!

"This went on all through the school year until the end, when it finally exploded. During the Memorial Day Parade at school, Sean was at the end of the line, being pushed in his wheelchair. I called up his teacher and said, 'I don't ever want to see Sean Allen pushed in his wheelchair at the end of a parade, isolated from the rest of his class! I know he has to be in the chair, but put him in among his peer group. How can you send him that kind of message?'

"She broke in and tried to fight with me. She said, 'It would've been more obvious if he were at the beginning.'

"I said, 'Didn't you hear me? I didn't say the beginning, I said somewhere in the group!'

"And she kept it up, even more. She said, 'Mrs. Allen, you're not working with us. What do you want, an education here, or do you want some kind of a social club?'

"We went back and forth with letters. I wrote to the principal, who responded that Sean wasn't toilet trained and shouldn't have been in school in the first place. The whole business of recess came up again. I mean, it was a bloody war."

"Did this ever get solved?"

Nick said, "Not for quite a while. It carried over into the first grade. The school recommended that Sean do an extra year called 'Primary One,' and we bought into this. It was the right placement for Sean at the time. I think he really did need the extra year, but the teacher had no business teaching small children, let alone those with disabilities. She was a real military type, and she did a number on Sean's self-esteem. He was at his lowest point then. He hated his teacher, he hated school, he'd cry in the mornings, and he wouldn't want to get out of bed. He'd say he felt sick. This woman had been teaching for thirty years, and she wasn't going to bend the system for anybody. She was rotten to all the kids, not just Sean."

"I guess you could say she was consistent," I said.

Lindy went on. "She started right at the top of the year by saying, 'Are you and your husband going to get bent out of shape if Sean can't go on field trips with the other kids? I can't hire a special bus just for him.'

"I said, 'Let me think about it and I'll get back to you.' I called the Special Education director for the area. He made it clear to me right away that the school was delighted to use their own bus that has a special lift built on it. Again, it's about learning how to access the system. The teacher didn't care enough about checking it out to find the right resource."

Nick said, "She just wasn't willing to change her routine to care about our son. There wasn't a liaison between Special Ed and the regular classroom teacher. We need that liaison because parents don't know all the answers. There ought to be a moderator to support the interaction between parents and the school."

"Can parents cry wolf too often?"

"Absolutely," Lindy responded. "But if we had a moderator, the cries of wolf would decrease and the system would work more appropriately. We learned that we had to work at one issue at a time. If Sean needed a computer, that's what we focused on. If Sean needed to be out at recess, that was the battle we fought. I don't fight for little things anymore. I try to pick the battles appropriately. In Sean's kindergarten year, we fought over too many things. We were scattered and not as organized as we should have been. We really didn't have a grasp as to how we should use the team of people involved in Sean's life."

"Who was involved in Sean's daily educational process?"

"Well, there was a classroom aid, and the classroom teacher," Lindy said, "and the Resource Room teacher. Then there was the physical therapist, the occupational therapist, the visual therapist, the school principal, the school counselor, the school nurse, the Special Ed director, and a few others thrown in. And that's just on the educational side of Sean's life, not the medical side. It was so confusing."

Nick said, "You wouldn't have believed the end-of-the-year meetings we went to. Those are required by law, but these people would hold a premeeting in advance, and already decide what we ought to talk about. Today it's a lot better, because now we are assumed as part of the team. In order for our son to have an appropriate education, there has to be an effective I.E.P.—that's an Individual Education Plan—and that plan has to be managed. Our team is operating better now, but I still think we need an educational liaison."

"Let me give you the strongest example that I can come up with," Lindy said. "During kindergarten period, the teacher placed a corral around Sean's desk to keep his attention on his work. I saw it as another way of making him different. I went crazy."

This hit me in the pit of my stomach. When I was a little boy, my parents had built a fence around my backyard. The idea was to keep me inside and keep the world outside. "Lindy, I can't believe you're telling me this. So what did you do?"

"I wrote to his teacher, 'He's disabled enough, and now you're making it worse.'

"But she said, 'Mrs. Allen, we've used those at schools all the time. It's not just for Sean Allen.'

"Well, I've been there a lot and I've never seen any other child involved in a corral setting. So I told her I was going to come to the classroom for the day and observe.

"She sent me a note back that said, 'You can come to my classroom for twenty minutes on Tuesday or Thursday morning.' And she even told me it was a rule.

"I called the School Committee and asked, 'Is that true, that I can only observe my son for twenty minutes? I can't spend an hour or two?' The School Committee said there was an archaic rule like that on the books. I stood outside, and I watched what was going on in that classroom. I checked out the time, and I was pissed. Exactly at nine-thirty I walked into that classroom. I stayed there precisely twenty minutes to make the point, no shorter, no longer. And this on-going crisis continued all through Sean's fill-in year. He still wasn't going out for recess. He was always behind on his papers because he would have to be pulled out of class to go to occupational or physical therapy. We just couldn't seem to get a handle on all this stuff. These people even had the nerve to say that Sean didn't want to go out for recess anyway."

"That's funny," I laughed. "People still talk about me like that. They even say when I'm in a group, 'What would he like to eat?' Instead of asking me directly. I guess that's the way it is for people with a disability."

Lindy went on. "I almost had a nervous breakdown that year. I lost fifteen pounds, I couldn't focus on anything. It was the single worst year of my life."

Nick said, "Lindy was so upset, she was even angry at me, because I was intimidated by the professionals. I think she started to doubt whether I was as committed to the issues as she was. I can remember nights when she'd just throw things around the house, and yell, and cry. We never came close to divorce, but it was a bad time. During Sean's kindergarten and extra year, we'd go to the school, and you could even see it on people's faces. We'd get dirty looks, or I'd hear other parents and teachers say, 'Here come those Allens.' With the success that Sean's having now, it's hard to believe it was that bad."

Lindy went on. "It was so bad with the corral, that I refused to sign Sean's Individual Education Plan, and that prompted the worst of all the meetings, when the team was brought together. This time, we got a professional Parent Advocate to carry our case forward. The Advocate contacted the school and asked them to do a study on how Sean was doing. We weren't trying to make things worse, we were just trying to get some professional help. But in retrospect, it was probably a mistake, because when we went to the meeting, everybody was upset."

Nick went on. "Prior to that meeting, I had called the Department of Education for the State of Massachusetts, and had spoken with an advocate, to ask some questions concerning Sean's education. We were not filing a complaint, but this guy contacted our Special Ed Director, who became so angry. Our Special Ed director started the meeting trying to cream me. He was screaming, 'Why did you call the Department of Education? There was no reason for you to do that. You should be communicating with the people who are interacting with your child!'"

"You know, on the one hand they were right," Lindy said. "But how can you communicate with people who have no sensitivity toward your son?"

Nick jumped in again. "I felt like I was in the middle of a lynch mob. Nobody was thinking about Sean. They were only thinking about how we were abusing the bureaucracy. Everybody was protecting their own turf. It was unbelievable."

Lindy couldn't contain herself. "I don't think we had to have so many people in the room. We could have just sat down with the Special Education director and worked it out. And so this was awful now. It was so complicated. This meeting should have been much simpler. It was the most humiliating experience of my life. I still can't look at some of those people, even now. It makes me cry to think about it. Some of those tears are anger, and some of those are tears of pain."

"We were so adversarial with everybody," Nick added. "Thank goodness it has turned around over the years. We're getting along now. Maybe we've learned to make the system work. We've also gained a level of acceptance because Sean has become a model student whom the school can point to with pride."

Lindy said, "I don't want to overdramatize or philosophize this, but the shocking thing about meetings like this for parents of Special-Needs kids is that nobody talks about the psychological areas, the philosophical areas, on behalf of the child. We talk only about solving the bureaucratic confusion. They even accused me of missing meetings or not keeping to the schedule. They weren't thinking about what was going on inside Sean or our feelings as human beings. It's simply a tough situation, because nobody is objective. I don't know if that part of the Special Education system will ever get better. But if we're ever going to see improvement, we need commitment. I'm not a teacher, I'm Sean Allen's parent. I suppose I'm a crisis manager, but I want professionals to want to be professionals. Sometimes I'd like to feel that the burden is being lifted, that competent people are truly involved in my son's life. Sometimes I want to be able to take a breath. I want my child to be independent. I don't know if Sean will ever get there, but I think it's possible if we can make this marriage of parents and professionals work."

"Lindy, you mentioned this idea of taking a breath. Do you ever get a break?"

"On the Cape we have a terrific respite system in which people come in and give us some time off. And we found this great sitter, Steve, who treats Sean like a little boy, and gives us some free time. We've even started to go to a movie, or take a picnic to the beach. I'm so grateful that this system exists. It's another example of making things work if you just know how to find the answers somewhere in the bureaucracy. I'm also grateful that I have so many good friends to communicate with. Sometimes I worry that Nick doesn't have that, but maybe men don't need it in the same way."

Nick laughed. "I have some good friends, but I'm able to get involved in my work, and in puttering around the house. I get breaks that way. And now, with our respite help, things are a lot better."

"Folks, let me go on with education. First grade, after the tragedy of all the meetings, it wasn't that bad, right? I mean, you told me before we started this that though his teacher wasn't the most dynamic person in the world, she didn't cause any crisis either, and she really did care about Sean."

Nick said, "That's right, Tom. Sean actually did pretty well academically, and he did start to socialize with other kids. I guess first grade was sort of a lull after the storm of the previous two years, but second grade was really the highlight, up to this point, in Sean's education. This was especially true when you consider that Sean had just had his big surgery that summer. He couldn't move around much, and he had to spend a lot of time in a wheelchair. In fact, when he first started school, we had to bring him there for only half-days. Every morning was a struggle because he didn't want to be there, and he didn't want to be in a wheelchair that he couldn't sit straight up in. It was really tough."

Nick went on. "A wonderful male influence came into Sean's life during the second grade: his teacher, Mr. LeClair. He started to do everything for Sean that we wanted and that Sean needed. He'd walk Sean out at recess. He'd say, 'Okay, they're playing dodgeball, and these are the adaptations I think can be achieved so that Sean can participate in the game.' He adapted the classroom so Sean could be with all the kids without the corral. And, at the end of the year, he wrote a personal report on his perception of Sean's development. I cannot say enough about this wonderful person."

Now I laughed. "It's great to hear you folks say something positive about someone in education."

Lindy corrected me on this. "Look, Tom, I think maybe we've given you the wrong impression. There are a lot of terrific people involved in the educational system, it's just that the system is so cumbersome and the needs of a Special Child are so complex, it's hard to find solutions. We haven't done everything right as parents, but Sean is our child and so we take it seriously. I've got to be careful here; again, I don't want to indicate that the professionals don't take it seriously, it's just that they don't necessarily know Sean the way we do."

Nick agreed. "I feel that we're well on the road to Sean's educational growth. His use of the computer, the A that he just got in math, the fact that his teachers think his papers are terrific are moving Sean forward educationally, and I think his future is bright."

"That's wonderful," I said. "But I guess now we ought to talk about whether that same sense of a bright future applies to the socialization process. Maybe that's the hardest part of all this."

"I think it is," Lindy said, "because it's the part that none of us can control."

"How early can we start talking about socialization?" I asked.

"I suppose right from birth," Lindy said. "Sean was a

grumpy baby, and my family always thought that it was colic and that he'd get over it. That probably conditioned their sense of who he was."

Nick added, "That's absolutely true. I think that certainly their sense of Sean was that he was a normal child because he looked normal, and by the time he was a year old and we learned about the cerebral palsy, people already had preconceptions about him. Then, when they came to understand that he had CP, I suppose they felt so sorry for him, they never could see him as anything but different."

Lindy laughed sarcastically. "You know it still happens now. Last week when we took my mom into the hospital for a cardiac checkup, one of the nurses asked her who had brought her in. My mom said, 'Oh, my daughter Connie; she's a teacher; and my daughter Lindy; she has a CP child.' Sean's not the only one who gets labeled; so do we. I can't overstate this issue of parent identity and its relationship to the identity of your child."

Nick said, "Every family has social dynamics, but when you add a child with a disability to the mix, there are all kinds of sub-text issues, like jealousy, discomfort, misunderstandings. I even think there's some hidden agenda that probably has some anger in it, too."

"Anger?" I asked.

"Yes, anger," Lindy said. "I remember one day when my brother Phil was talking to me about Sean. He just couldn't handle the situation so he became like the nurse in the hospital, when Sean was born. He said, 'Melinda, Sean is going to be just fine.' I lost it. If you ask Phil today, he'd feel awful about it. But still, in families those issues happen."

"So going on with this theme, how did Sean react to people early in his life?"

"It was tough," Nick said. "From the beginning, Sean was always more comfortable with adults. I think he felt safer, because since he was only crawling, he couldn't move out of the way when other kids were playing too rough. Now it seems so appropriate to me that when the doctors talk about how Sean crawls, they call it the "battle crawl." That's probably the way he perceived it. So he really didn't have much interaction with other children at the beginning."

"Lindy, when it did happen, who did he play with?"

"Interestingly, he chose to play with little girls. I think it was because their play was gentler, and he wasn't afraid of being stepped on or pushed down. I think playing with girls helped his communications skills, making him more verbal because they're more communicative early on."

"So how did you support the expansion of his social skills?"

Lindy had an easy answer. "It's up to parents," she said. "Parents have to be willing to find out what their child can do in a way that makes it fun for other kids to share, and then promote the hell out of it."

Nick said, "We're back to that advocacy theme again."

"That's true," Lindy went on. "But in this case, you've got to be sensitive to find out where your child's interests lie, and how those interests can be promoted. Now that's not true for all disabilities. Some are just too complicated, but in Sean's case, we really could get involved in helping him interact. For example, he was interested in music, and the Cape Cod Conservatory offered a class for kids his age. So I signed him up with a couple of his friends, Jimmy and Kari, and I took them every Wednesday afternoon. He did it for two years. It wasn't necessarily the best experience, but we got through it, and I think it did enhance Sean's social and musical interests. It was a group lesson, and he probably could have used more individual time, but I'm still glad we did it.

"We have to keep pushing the process of integration forward. For example, let's say that it's a nice, sunny day, and Sean is going to have a friend over who also enjoys the beach. They can bring a ball with them, and if it's the right kind of ball, big enough and soft enough, they can play together. Now I'll pack plenty of snacks, because I've learned that attracts other children. And so that's how we draw kids in. I guess to be fair, the socialization has to be planned. One of my biggest disappointments is that other parents do not invite Sean to their homes. I told his teacher for next year, 'You know, he has not been invited to one person's house at any time this year.' She just couldn't believe it because teachers think of him as being popular. Yet he is never invited. It's one thing for people to think of a child as exceptional, it's another for them not to treat him as an exception. Next year, I decided to take a different course with the teachers. I've asked them to tell me as soon as Sean finds a child in the class that he is relating to. I'll make sure I invite him over and I'll even call the family and suggest that sometimes Sean and I go over there. The boys can play and we'll have coffee. I've learned that I have to be pushy."

"Nick, I suppose you'll also have to always be the participating dad, right?"

"I'm actually looking forward to that, Tom. It's great to be involved. We can never get away from remembering his special needs, so I just have to stay a part of all of it. I'm glad that's the way it is, because I missed some of that with my own dad."

Lindy had her hand on her head again. "One of the toughest times in any parent's life is when you try to set up a play situation, and everything goes wrong. I remember when I've had kids over, and I was tired. Sean was inside watching television, and the kids were playing outside, and I wondered, what am I doing it for? I baked the cookies, popped the popcorn and rented the movies, but the kids played outside while Sean watched television inside."

"Has Sean reacted to that?" I asked.

"No. That's when I get angry at him. I'll say, 'If you want to have friends over, then you get out there and play with them.

You guys work it out, because I'm not going to be watching what the other child is doing outside, and what you're doing inside. So you people solve it.' And then he interacts and sometimes it comes out okay."

"Have there been any social highlights or successes?"

Nick said, "Yes, Sean has a new friend, Brad."

"Well remember this, Nick," I said. "It only takes one. I had Billy Hannon. He was my neighborhood friend, and he created the interaction for me. He facilitated my involvement with other kids. I hope Brad can do that for Sean. Lindy, is Sean playing at Brad's house ever?"

"Well, Brad is part of a single-parent family. It hasn't been easy yet, but I hope it gets better."

"Since Sean has made this friend, has his general social life improved?"

They were both delighted to talk about this. Nick said, "Recently, at a family gathering, Sean was with his cousins, Adam and Ryan. Sean wasn't the odd guy out! Ryan and Sean both love sports, and Adam isn't as involved. And on that day, Sean and Ryan played and Adam was the outsider. Now I don't want to see any child be the outsider, but it was fantastic to see Sean playing."

Lindy said, "You know the same thing happened with the rest of our family that day. It involved my brothers Phil and Billy. It was late in the afternoon on Easter Sunday. We had our dinner, and the guys decided that after the Easter Egg Hunt they'd all go to Eagle Pond—that's a sanctuary—and have a good walk to digest the food. It's about a mile around the pond. Some of it is tough going, and we thought it would be impossible for Sean. But we let him go, and we stayed at home. Two years ago, we would have been saying, 'Which one of us goes, you or me?' But this time, we let them go. They walked around the whole pond, and Phil came home and said, 'Sean was unbelievable. I didn't carry him. Somehow he sucked it up and did it. I kept saying to him, 'Get going like Johnny Kelly, the great marathon runner.'

"And Sean kept saying, 'I can do it, I'm Seanie Kelly and I can run this marathon!'

"I think that knocked my brother out. So we already are beginning to see some change. Just the idea that he would say, 'Bye, mom and dad' and go off on his own is incredible to us. You know when we left him yesterday, he handled it. He didn't mind staying with mom and dad."

"Sean is also part of the Kettleleers Clinic," Nick said proudly.

"You mean, the team that plays baseball in Cotuit; the young guys who hope to be pros and have the college league there?"

"That's right," Nick said. "They run a clinic every summer, and Sean wanted to sign up for it."

"How is he going to do that?" I asked.

"It kind of beats me," Nick said. "But he feels he can be a participant. I took him yesterday, for the first day of practice. He might just pull this off. The coach was great. Every time they'd have the other kids run laps, the coach would pick a different course for Sean. They'll probably have him use a designated pusher so he can sit at home plate in his wheelchair and hit the ball and then be pushed to the bases. Maybe they'll have to come up with an adaptive situation for him to play in the outfield. But he really wants to interact with other kids in this setting. We're nervous as hell, but if he can make this happen, we really are beginning to see the light at the end of the tunnel."

"Do you agree with that, Lindy?" I asked.

"I do, Tom. But there is another issue that we're facing. And that's the question of whether Sean can accept that we believe he'll have to use a wheelchair at some point, on a more consistent basis."

"That really is a problem," I said. "My friend Mike Rantz teaches skiing for us up at the National Sport Center for the Disabled in Winter Park, Colorado. Mike has cerebral palsy, and he refused to use a chair all of his life, no matter how severe his limitations were."

"That is what I'm worried about," Lindy said. "Sean seems to be committed to walking."

"Well," I laughed, "how can we criticize that when he just completed his first mile marathon. So do you agree," I asked Lindy, "you're beginning to see the light at the end of the tunnel?"

"I do. I think Sean has stabilized educationally. Physically, we probably won't have another major crisis until the middle of adolescence. And socially, he's making progress. I don't know how much he'll make, but we do see some."

"So what does that mean for you two?" I asked.

"What do you mean?" Lindy said.

"Well, would you ever consider the possibility of having another child?"

There was an awkward pause. They didn't know it, but I knew they had taken each other's hand.

"I figured you'd ask about that, Tom," Lindy said quietly.

Nick went on. "We're thinking about it. For the first time, we're really thinking about it."

I jumped right in. "I think it would be great. I think Sean would be a tremendous older brother and a wonderful influence on any new person that came into the world. I hope you'll keep considering this possibility. A lot of your issues are getting easier. You're letting yourselves begin to enjoy free time. You're using the educational system more appropriately. And maybe, Lindy, you're beginning to feel some of that breathing space you talked about."

"I am," she said. "It's a wonderful feeling. I felt a little awkward in the beginning, coming over here to be with you and Patty. I didn't know how this conversation would turn out. But I feel great about what we've shared."

"So do I. I've known both of you for a long time, and I'm so proud of you. I'm so proud you're Sean's parents. You reinforce the idea that people don't know how much love and courage they truly possess until they're tested."

We had a great lunch and rode back on the ferry together. We had talked so much that everybody was quiet. We were just enjoying the feeling that all of us were participating in the life of a Special Child, and he was moving down the road toward a challenged, but bright, future.

CHAPTER

Robin and Bob

IN CHAPTER ONE, I wrote with surprise and maybe even shock when I began to learn how difficult my mother's life had been as the parent of a blind child. I suppose I thought that I knew everything there was to know about blindness. Why not? I was blind. But though I had done very well learning about how to be blind, I had no understanding about the life presented to a parent with a blind child.

Consequently, when I met Robin and Bob Rosso, I was shaken as I came to understand how complicated raising their nine-year-old blind son has been.

As in the case of all the parents in this book, the Rossos are aware that they must be parent advocates, but Robin Rosso has taken it a step further. She believes that in order to gain the life she knows is possible for her son, she must be a revolutionary, fighting battles with the system and never giving up her sense of what's possible in Jim's future. A letter I received from her at the end of our first day of meetings makes us clearly aware of her role as a soldier.

> *Raising a non-disabled, regular-education child is like fighting the Gulf War. The great majority of these children are going to make it, just like our soldiers did. These children are going to live independent lives, achieve some degree of career success, or at least obtain employment, marry, raise families— all the usual things.*
>
> *Raising a disabled, special-education child is more like the Allied Invasion of Normandy. Many, perhaps most, aren't going to make it in the same way. They will end up with a lesser degree of independence and career success, and their "families" may be quite different. As Jim's mom, I'm perhaps a bit like General Eisenhower. I know the risks and the statistical casualties, but I can't dwell on them because my son is one of the Marines who's going to hit the beach on that fateful day. I must keep pumped up and optimistic. I must believe with all my heart that Jim is going to be one of the ones who will make the beachhead, or I'll lose the courage and motivation to go on.*
>
> *Talking with you is like talking with one of the Marines who made it. You're talented, extraordinarily capable, and a well-trained soldier, and you've reached the beachhead. If there was no Tom Sullivan to tell the story of success, we generals wouldn't have the heart to continue the invasion. Thank you for making it to that beachhead, Tom, and thank Patty, too. That you made it means it can be done, and that's our inspiration, motivation, and ultimate objective.*

Our interview took place at the Rosso home in the Conejo Valley in Southern California on a Saturday afternoon, while their blind son, Jim, and their daughter, Lindsey, were visiting their grandparents.

"I know from our telephone conversation that you both went to the University of Southern California and passed the bar the first time around, becoming lawyers. Do you practice law, Robin?"

"Not recently, Tom. Sometimes I backseat for Bob in the office when he is busy, but family has to be the dominant part of my life."

"How soon after you got married did you have Lindsey?" I asked. I could feel that Robin and Bob looked at each other. There was a pause.

And Robin said, "Well, Lindsey wasn't our first child. I got pregnant three and a half years after we got married, with Andy. Andy was our first."

I could sense that maybe they didn't want to talk about this, but I had a responsibility to ask. "Andy isn't with us?"

"No, Andy's not with us," Bob said.

"It was a normal pregnancy," Robin explained. "I delivered Andy by C-section, and the next day all the grandparents showed up. Andy was the first grandchild for both sets of grandparents, and he was perfect—this blond baby with big beautiful blue eyes. But the whole world fell apart when the pediatrician came in the morning of the second day. I was still feeling the effects of Demerol. I don't know why I was on such a big painkiller, but my brain wasn't doing very well. It was trying to function and I was struggling. They didn't call Bob. I couldn't understand that; he was only twenty minutes away. The pediatrician looked at me and said, 'Mrs. Rosso, your baby is sick.'

"'Okay, what's he got,' I asked, 'the flu?' Now it happened that the doctor was a guy of very few words. I said, 'Well, does he have a cold?'

"'No.'

"'Well, what are his symptoms?' And no one was telling me. All I got were yes and no answers. So I started thinking, I'm not asking the right questions. I had a teacher in law school who said if you don't ask the right questions, you don't get the right answers. So I said, 'Is my baby going to die?'

"He said, 'Yes, I think so.'

"I went into shock. I called Bob, I called my dad, and everybody came."

"And then what happened, Bob?" I asked.

"The doctor explained that Andy was suffering from hypoplastic left heart syndrome. One of the four chambers of the heart was not properly developed. There is a flap that doesn't close until after the child's birth, so the condition doesn't show up for twenty-four to thirty-six hours."

"I bet this becomes important later on, right?" I asked.

"It does," Robin said, "because Jim's blindness didn't show up until much later."

"So what happened next?"

"An incredible pediatric cardiologist came in to visit us," Bob said. "I will always be grateful to him. He was a great doctor and a compassionate human being. About thirty-six hours went by and then we got the word that Andy had died."

"Bob, you skipped a lot," Robin interjected. "They did a full heart catheterization, and tell him about you and Andy and the incubator."

"When I reached inside," Bob said, "Andy hung onto my fingers like he was grabbing for life. I couldn't do anything to help him, and he died."

"So can you remember when you decided to consider getting pregnant again with Lindsey?"

"Actually, there was another baby before Lindsey," Robin said, "but we lost him at about one and a half months of that pregnancy. It started to make me crazy. I started to think that maybe I wasn't supposed to have babies."

"But we were still optimists," Bob said. "We didn't wait

very long to have Lindsey. She was also born by cesarean, but she was a perfect baby."

"You say that with a lot of pride, Dad."

Bob laughed. "That's how I feel. I feel proud of Lindsey. She has been a remarkable child. I never analyzed this before, but after losing Andy and then the miscarriage, I really wanted a girl. And I suppose when we had Lindsey, part of my dream was completed. We're so much alike, maybe that's why I have always been comfortable with her."

"What is she like?" I asked.

Bob smiled. "Well she's smarter than us, first of all."

"And what about her hobbies and interests?"

"Boys," they said together.

Robin went on. "She likes things that are cute and feminine. She's also into cheerleading and tennis—until she gets hot and sweaty—but she is really very much an internalized girl, and she is one of those kids, maybe because she has a brother with a disability, who totally knows herself."

"What else should I know about her?"

"It's her sensitivity," Robin said. "She seems to be able to look inside things and understand the fundamental truths. She is just special."

"That's wonderful," I said. "Now I suppose you were going to go into the baby business again."

"Oh, no question," Bob said. "After Lindsey's birth we were excited."

"So you got pregnant with Jim. Any complications?"

"None." Bob was emphatic. "It was a perfect pregnancy and then we had Jim."

I almost could hear an audible sigh in his voice. "We all know that Jim is blind, but I suppose it's important for me to tell the readers what his condition is, I mean, his actual medical condition."

Robin said, "He has Leber's congenital amaurosis. Leber is the name of the man who discovered the disease."

"What is Leber's? Can you describe it?"

Robin tried. "The eye is all there. It looks fine, but when the doctor does the electroretinogram he finds that the retina just isn't functioning."

Bob tried to help. "The light gets as far as the retina, but it doesn't transmit to the optic nerve."

Robin said, "It makes me believe that if they can transplant retinal tissue, maybe someday Jim will see."

"Robin, when I wrote the introduction to this book, I described my mother's feelings when she found out I was blind. How did you react? You brought Jim home. Everybody was excited. It's a seemingly healthy boy. Even Lindsey was excited. So you started the process of being a mom. Take me down the road of discovery, when you began to suspect that Jim was blind."

"You know, Tom, there is something inside you—you can't put your finger on—it is an animal instinct. You can feel it. A mother knows that something is wrong. You might not admit that you know because it is so deep, so down in there, it's beyond subconscious. It's a primal thing. The bonding isn't quite right. When we were home, I was sitting on the sofa, feeding him his bottle. I was looking at him and thinking, 'This child doesn't look at me, he doesn't like me.' "

"How old was he?" I asked.

"Just a couple of weeks."

"But, Robin, at that stage the eye isn't fully functioning yet."

"I had a subliminal thought that there might be something wrong with this baby's eyes. So I'd look at Lindsey and talk to her. I just didn't want to deal with those eyes. And it was only a week later, when the pediatrician saw the nystagmus, the twitching movements in Jim's eyes, that he sent us to Children's Hospital to see the pediatric ophthalmologist, who was head of the department."

I was amazed. "You know, folks, this happened so much earlier than it did in my life. I don't think my parents knew that I was blind until I was about six months old."

Robin added, "Well, Jim's blindness wasn't confirmed until much later. I was so naive. I wasn't so upset when the pediatrician said that Jim might have an eye problem. I thought it might be something simple like crossed eyes."

Bob said, "That's not the way I remember it. When I got back to my office after lunch, my secretary said, 'You'd better call Robin. She's upset.'"

"Bob, I wasn't upset. I was concerned, but I don't think I really perceived that there would be any possibility of blindness. If anything, I was upset because we had the whole weekend before we could see the ophthalmologist."

"So the next important moment was that visit?" I asked.

"It was," Bob said, "and I can remember it clearly. The ophthalmologist looked at Jim's eyes and then started dictating a long letter to the pediatrician. When the examination was finished, he turned to us and said, 'I don't think there is anything really wrong with his eyes other than the nystagmus. He doesn't seem to be tracking correctly, but I think that will work out as he begins to mature. Let's see what happens as he develops. Come and see me in a couple of months. By that time, I'm sure he will be tracking correctly.'"

Robin added, "Now I remember the last sentence of the letter that he wrote to the pediatrician; it said, 'There is the remote possibility of Leber's, but the likelihood was the more benign diagnosis of congenital nystagmus, and 20/30 to 20/40 vision.' So we took him home."

"Between the time that you brought Jim home and the time that you realized that he was going to be blind, were you feeling tension? Were you talking about all this?"

Bob laughed. "I suppose this is where the dark humor comes in. Robin, tell Tom about Christy."

"Christy was a little girl who lived across the street, and it happened that she had one eye. As far as I was concerned, she and her mother were experts on blindness. So we used to take a flashlight and wave it in front of Jim's face and I'd say, 'Oh, he's tracking. Look, see how he's following the light? He's doing better.' Then I would do the same thing on weekends when Bob was home. I'd say, 'Bob, come here, look, he's tracking better. Christy says so.'"

"This has to be an example of mother's optimism, right?"

"I think every mother has to be optimistic; I kept up this level of hope for four or five months. We even saw the ophthalmologist again, and he didn't change the diagnosis. I never understood why he didn't run the electroretinogram and the visually evoked response test sooner."

Bob interrupted. "But even if he didn't, I knew the jig was up. Too much time was going by, and Jim wasn't using his eyes. Robin was upset, but she didn't say anything. Nobody said anything." Bob took her hand. "Robin, I guess I figured you knew. I tried to help."

"I think that's right, Robin," I said. "You know we have been talking about parenting instincts being even more developed than doctors' skills and I'm convinced that's true. It's just that, early, you don't trust those instincts."

Bob said, "I don't want to sound like I knew everything. The truth is, I tried to convince myself that Jim was tracking. I let Robin convince me. But I was never really convinced."

"Then how would you describe your state of mind?"

"We were frantic," Robin said. "I started running around to all kinds of doctors. I went to the Jules Stein Institute at U.C.L.A. and consulted with an ophthalmologist there. I asked everyone I could think of about the nystagmus. I probably would have talked to strangers on the street about it if I thought they knew anything. We weren't thinking in terms of Leber's yet because statistically it was such a long shot. You get kind of crazy as a parent during this time because nothing is conclusive. We finally went down to U.S.C. and had all the appropriate tests run. A radiologist, basically a tech doctor, did the testing. I probably wasn't fair, but the ophthalmologist was out of the country and I didn't want to wait for the test results. I said, 'Look you're going to have to call the police to get rid of us if you don't tell us the truth right now.'"

"I was absolutely sure Jim couldn't see," Bob said, "but I was holding on to that ray of hope. I had seen on the printout that the needle on the machine didn't move when they put light on Jim's eyes. So I hammered away at this tech doc and we'll never forget his words: 'Mr. and Mrs. Rosso, your son doesn't know the difference between day and night.'"

"I went crazy," Robin said. "It was awful. It wasn't his job to tell us whether Jim was going to be blind or sighted, so he wasn't prepared with what to say. At any rate, Jim has always known the difference between day and night, maybe not the way we do, but he has always known the difference."

"So what happened next?" I asked.

"We got home and Robin kept saying, 'It will be all right, it will be all right.' It sounded like a mantra. I decided to go running on the track. Now, I run on the track all the time. I usually run four miles in 32 or 33 minutes. This time, I looked at my watch at the end of four miles and it said 28:10. I guess adrenaline or emotion can be pretty powerful."

"What did you do now, Bob? You were running and Robin was repeating a mantra."

"Well, I did the same thing that I did when Andy was born. I went back to work. I guess that's how I cope with stress—exercise and work."

"And what about you, Robin?"

"I remember lying in bed the first night crying. I kept thinking, 'I'll never be able to send Jim to a private school. He'll have to go to public school, and maybe then he won't get into a good college.' What an absurd thought, and yet it was based on my sense of how life was for *me,* because I hadn't been exposed to blindness before. I certainly didn't know what it was like to raise a blind child, and then there was something else. Somebody had said that blindness could be involved with other disabilities, and I kept thinking that's the one thing I can't handle. I can't cope with mental retardation."

Bob said, "And that was one of the issues that came up later about Jim. So you can understand that one of Robin's most basic fears became a reality."

"Our school district's teacher for the visually handicapped was really the first person to help," Robin said. "She suggested that we try to get Jim into the Mommy and Me infant development program at Easter Seals. It's a little complicated because you have to be able to show that your child is not only blind, but at risk of being developmentally delayed. The medical literature on Leber's amaurosis said it can have all kinds of ramifications. Some doctors believe you can have renal failure, you can be deaf, and that there is retardation connected to the issue. So Jim got into the Easter Seals program and I started the next stage of craziness. This was my 'I'll-read-everything-in-the-literature-and-meet-everyone-connected-with-blindness stage.' I remember calling bookstores and asking them to send me books on blindness, and store owners said, 'Well, should I send one or two or do you have choices in mind?' and I'd say, 'No, just send everything you have,' and they'd come by the boxes. I tried to make Bob read everything."

Bob laughed. "We had a lot of reading to do, and I suppose I let Robin do it. Then a friend ran a computer check at the hospital library and got us all the medical articles ever written on Leber's."

"How old was Jim at this time?" I asked.

"Oh, he was about eight months. Then we took him back to

visit the pediatric ophthalmologist. That was an interesting conversation. The doctor said that the hardest part of his job was telling parents that their child is going to be blind. I probably should have asked him why he didn't give us an earlier diagnosis, but he is really an incredibly good man, so I didn't. I do remember him saying, 'Those Leber's children are delightful. You will have a delightful child,' and he referred us to the Blind Children's Center, which begins the next stage of the saga."

They both laughed, but I could hear some strain in the sound.

Robin went on. "I remember going to the Blind Children's Center the first time and meeting the child developmental specialist. She started by saying, 'Jimmy is a cute baby, and here are things you need to do to encourage his development. Just play these block games with him and get him sitting up and exploring. Help him start moving around, and everything will be fine.' I remember thinking it couldn't be that cut and dried. I knew it couldn't be that simple. But I suppose I walked out of the first meeting with a sense of hope, and a lot of confidence in her knowledge. She had a medical diploma from a European university on her wall, and she had worked with blind children for over twenty years, so I figured she knew everything there was to know about them. I thought if I did what she said, everything would be all right and Jim would be a successful blind person like the ones I'd read about in blind autobiographies. You know, that's what parenting is all about when you have a child with a disability. You're always on a constant path to affirm hope. That's how we survive."

"But hope doesn't last long," I said.

"Hope lasts forever." It was Bob speaking now. "But then reality jumps up and bites you on the butt. Actually, it attacks your heart."

"And the reality was," Robin said, "that the developmental specialist began to tell me that blindness carried with it developmentally delaying issues. I wasn't even willing to consider the possibility that Jim was behind. That might have been naive, but it's that optimism that has gotten me through."

"Robin, who's naive here, the parents or the professionals?"

"I don't know, Tom. I suppose we all are. The professionals tend to label blind kids developmentally delayed. They don't get the learning supplied by sight and it takes more time for them to catch up developmentally. But a lot of visually impaired children, especially those born totally blind like Jim, just follow a different path. Still, somehow, they all come out at the same place. For example, Jim never crawled. He just walked. And other kids crawl backwards because they are afraid of hitting their heads."

"I was a butt scooter," I laughed. "My mother said that I liked to get my feet out in front of me and then scoot along the ground because it was safe."

Robin was animated now. "That's right, and that's why kids don't sit up as early when they're blind. They're not visually stimulated. But if a child gets labeled 'developmentally delayed' early, it's really difficult to shake. We've had to deal with that all the way through the system: the difference between what we now call visually handicapped (VH), or just blind, and multi-handicapped (MH), which often translates to mentally handicapped in the system's unwritten code. This is the great parent crisis when you have a blind child, because it determines the educational track your child will be on. Jim wasn't a physically active child, so he didn't follow any of the developmental charts. I took him to the developmental specialist at the Blind Children's Center for six months and he wasn't carrying out certain behaviors on schedule. This indicated to her that his problems might be far more complicated than they really turned out to be."

"Explain all this, please," I said.

"Well, you know what's remarkable, Tom? All this happened on a day that your wife was at the Blind Children's Center talking about what your life had been like. I had an appointment with the developmental specialist before I could attend Patty's talk. I had a whole list of questions for Patty about how you got to Harvard and what kinds of things I needed to do for Jim so that he could go to a wonderful school. I wanted to know what marriage would be like, and what kind of a father Jim would be. I believed the sky was the limit."

Bob said, "You even made us go all the way back to Boston because you believed that all of the successful blind people you had read about went to Perkins School for the Blind. So we flew to the east coast and even checked out colleges in the area. You started to write down the names and addresses of blind college students because you wanted to develop a correspondence with them to get advice for Jim."

Robin sighed. "Sometimes parents are wacko."

"No they're not," I said, "they are loving, and I wish there were more of them like you two. Anyway, let's get on with the feelings of the developmental specialist. So Jim wasn't following her schedule, right?"

Robin said, "That's right. And she said, 'I'm very concerned about Jimmy.'

"'How concerned are you?' I asked.

"She repeated, 'I'm very concerned.'

"I said, 'It's because he's not doing all those things on your developmental charts, right?'

"And she said, 'I'm very concerned about Jimmy.'

"I looked her straight in the eye and asked 'Do you think Jim is mentally retarded?'

"She said, 'I'm very concerned about Jimmy.'

"And I thought, 'I've heard this kind of conversation before when Andy died. I'm going to get the truth from this woman.' I asked her again, 'Do you think Jim is mentally retarded?' and I said it loud so that I knew she could hear me.

"And she said, 'I'm very concerned about Jimmy,' and then she said, 'Robin, you should be grateful. There are other mothers around here whose children are in wheelchairs and are handicapped in many ways, and these children are worse off than Jimmy.'

"I left her office crying. And then I had to go into the room where Patty was and I had this list of questions about going to Harvard rolled up on a piece of paper in my hand, and I couldn't ask them. I just couldn't ask them."

Her voice broke and I knew she was crying, so we waited. "Bob, where were you in all this? What did Robin tell you?"

"She came home that night and told me what the specialist had said, and I didn't believe it. I knew she was a professional, but I thought it was much too early to make that kind of diagnosis. I told Robin that we needed to wait and see."

"This was the worst moment in our lives," Robin said. "This was a disaster. This was a tornado, an earthquake, the worst kind of hurricane, our house burning down around us. It was awful beyond words."

"You two seem to see this moment differently. Is that true, Bob?"

"I think I'd already gotten to the point where I was saying, 'How many different ways can you get screwed?' Sometimes when you're dealing with what you perceive as a tragedy, I think you just get to a place where you deal with life day to day. It's almost as if fate keeps hitting you hard in the stomach, you don't feel it after a while. I suppose the difference in parents is that some keep trying, and some just quit. Really because of Robin, we kept trying, and also because I had other realities to deal with. I had a law practice to run, there were bills that had to be paid, and there was Lindsey. I remember that Jim's problems got more and more complicated, and I just kept trying to cope."

"I think all parents do that. I know with my own children that's how Patty and I function. It's probably the best part of the marriage." They both agreed.

Then Robin surprised me. "That was the strength of the marriage, Tom, but it was certainly the worst time. I don't know what was going on in my head, but after the developmental specialist said those things to me, I was beyond grief, without hope, just empty, empty. I had found a wonderful psychotherapist who specialized in counseling families with disabled members, and who was going blind herself because of retinitis pigmentosa. During one session I said, 'One can live successfully with blindness. I mean, look at Tom Sullivan'—I was always quoting you—'but mentally retarded and blind, that's not possible. So,' I said, 'I brought this child into the world, I'm going to take responsibility for this. I'm taking this out of God's hands; it's no longer His choice. I'm going to risk going to hell, but this child is not going to live in this world without me and be stuck in some institution with people who don't care about him, and that's it. I've had it. I know exactly what I'm going to do. Last week, a kid drove over the guardrail on the Conejo grade—that's perfect for me—and people will think it's an accident. And so I'm going to do this unless you can give me one good reason why I shouldn't.'"

"Bob, did you know this was happening?"

"She'd tell me these things, but I thought I knew Robin pretty well and that it was all just a reaction. I figured she had to let off emotional steam."

"You could go to work every day and not be worried about it?"

"No, no, no. I worried about it, but not in terms of Robin really doing anything drastic. I worried about her stability, but I knew she was seeing a competent professional, so I was confident she'd work it out."

"Thank goodness the therapist was so perceptive," Robin

continued. "She said, 'I'm not going to tell you not to drive off the road with Jim. I'm not going to give you one good reason. In the first place, let's be rational about this. The fact of the matter is it might not kill you, it might just injure you, then you're really in trouble. What do you do then? I think we need to give it six more months. Let's see what develops. You know, he's only a year old and you never can tell what might happen in six months. You might feel differently then. Robin, it's surprising how much children can change in six months.'

"And I bought into this idea. I suppose I was looking for a life raft. In retrospect, she did an extraordinary job. I'm sure all she could do at that point was buy time. Still, it's amazing the thoughts that went through my mind. I felt guilty and wanted to blame myself. The therapist knew she needed to give me options and time, because adults really can't tell other adults what to do. In six months, I was able to think things out, and heal a little from the trauma of the developmental specialist's devastating diagnosis. Even if things had turned out differently than they did, and Jim had more than one disability, the six months would have given me time to realize that Jim is the little boy I love, and his life is worthwhile no matter what."

"Robin, are you telling me that doctors and educators generally are not sensitive enough?"

"Tom, if I could say one thing to doctors, educators, and all professionals who work with families of children with disabilities it's this: they need to know their power and the effect their words can have on these families. Predictions about a child's future should not be given without great circumspection and an extraordinary degree of sensitivity for the parents' feelings. If parents lose hope, everything is lost. That's when the potential for divorce or even something as horrible as suicide becomes a reality. The specialist at the Blind Children's Center saw Jim only for short periods of time within the confines of her office. She didn't come to our home to observe him in his own environment where he was most comfortable. On the basis of these limited observations, she said he had multiple disabilities. At a year old, I believe he was just too young to go through any kind of meaningful formal testing. I gave her diagnosis too much credibility because of her medical background and long experience working with blind children. But I suppose I should have thought it through more rationally rather than let my emotions take over."

"How did you hold up, Bob?" I asked.

"I love Robin, and I had exercise and my work and there was Lindsey, and that was my way of coping day to day. When I think of our lives today, I mean the way it is now, I'm so glad we survived."

"But survival is day to day," I said. "What did you do next?"

"I decided to take Jim back to Easter Seals. An occupational therapist there is one of my 'A' list people. In the Mommy and Me therapy sessions, there were a number of children with Down syndrome and they were happy, and then there were some children with cerebral palsy, who also enjoyed therapy, and then there was Jim, who screamed the whole time. He didn't want to ride on the swing, he didn't want to go down the slide, he didn't want to be there, and he made it very clear to everyone. So I said to the O.T., 'When I bring Jim here, I need you to get involved. He doesn't scream as much with you. Will you do the therapy with him?'

"And she said, 'Robin, it's time that we start looking at the donut, not the hole. Now I'm going to point out to you things about Jim that you should view as positives. I think we need to start there.'"

Bob was talking now. "She really was a remarkable person. She was an occupational therapist by training, but she had no experience with blindness. She dealt with Jim as a human being, as she said, 'looking at the donut, not the hole.'"

Robin said, "There aren't many people like that terrific

O.T., but I've met a few. All of my 'A' list people have this natural instinct, and they are not limited by charts and graphs and the restrictions of science or empirical studies. The Blind Children's Center wanted me to bring Jim back to them, so I walked a tightrope between the Center and Easter Seals. I made a deal with the Center that their child developmental specialist wouldn't be directly involved with Jim. She could observe him, but that was all. I stayed in the Mommy and Me program at the Center, but I never interacted with the developmental specialist, until the end of Jim's time there."

"What happened?" I asked.

"I came as close to getting an apology from her as anybody has. She said to me that she was delighted with Jim's verbal skills and his progress. And I said, 'You mean that you no longer think Jim's retarded?'

"She didn't answer directly, but said, 'I'm not concerned about Jimmy anymore because of his verbal ability.'"

"Tom, I've also observed that these kids get categorized," Bob added. "Jim got labeled by the developmental specialist as MH right at the beginning, and it's unfortunate. The special-education community is so small that kids carry these labels with them. I think Robin, particularly, has spent much of Jim's life trying to correct this very serious misconception on the part of the specialists."

"That's right," Robin nearly screamed. "I've spent years trying to make people understand that there shouldn't be a label perception. Because of Jim's academic progress, and his ability to read and write braille and do math, the MH label is finally buried. And it never should have been put on him in the first place, particularly by professionals, who should have known better."

"I think that's true, Robin," I said, "but I was closely involved with the Blind Children's Center, and it seems to me that

Jim just fell through the cracks and that you had a personality conflict with the specialist."

Bob said, "And then we went to San Francisco and saw a pediatric neuro-ophthalmologist. He's an expert, Robin told me, in Leber's and has really done more to understand these children than anyone else in the country."

"From the minute I met him, I liked him," Robin said. "There's another 'A' list person. I'd been reading all these medical articles, and it was terrible because the European doctors were saying, 'Leber's children can have deafness, renal failure, and potentially mental retardation, not just blindness; complication after complication.' Now good old Leber discovered two different diseases, one was Leber's congenital amaurosis and the other was Leber's optic nerve hypoplasia. These are two totally different genetic tracks, two totally different diseases. Unfortunately, some doctors confuse the two.

"So as I read these articles, with all that going on and really nobody knowing much about these diseases, I became more and more confused and upset. Six or seven different diseases may be involved. But the doctor in San Francisco really understood Leber's. In his article he said that he had seen thirty-one American children, and as far as he was concerned, mental retardation is not associated with Leber's amaurosis, at least not in North America. However, some children may have balance problems and low muscle tone, caused by hypoplasia of the cerebellar vermis. I thought that sounded like Jim and so we had him take a CAT scan. From the minute I met this neuro-ophthalmologist, I knew that he was tremendous. The first thing I noticed was that his shoes weren't polished, which immediately made me feel he was a down-to-earth human being. He was not one of those spit and polish, egocentric doctors."

Bob noted, "I guess I should tell you here that I didn't actually go up to San Francisco with Robin. Her mom did."

"So I suppose I should ask you, Bob, if this was important."

"I thought Robin was chasing windmills. She just had to know what Jim's condition was. She used to wake me up in the middle of the night, sometimes asking, 'Do you think he's mentally retarded?' We were back to the mantra again. She was using all the big medical terms. She became an expert."

"You did, Robin," I said. "But I suppose that's what parents have to do with children who have disabilities. They become advocates and experts."

"I'm glad I did, Tom," Robin was announcing now, "because if I hadn't I don't know where Jim would be."

Now Bob and I were agreeing with her. "So what did the doctor say when you got to San Francisco?"

"After studying the CAT scan, he said, 'He doesn't have hypoplasia of the cerebellar vermis, so we can take that away.' I asked him about his article and if he still stood by his thesis that mental retardation isn't associated with Leber's amaurosis. He said he hadn't seen any exceptions yet. 'Well, guess what,' I said, 'I think you're going to have your first case. I mean, Jim's not doing anything on the developmental charts.'

"He gave me so much confidence. He said, 'These babies don't do anything on those kinds of charts. Just wait awhile, it will come out okay.' And so every year I call him to see if he still stands by his thesis. And every year I see Jim making progress and I know he was right."

"I'm jumping ahead," I said, "and I know it's a tough question, but where do you think Jim is now?"

"I think he's got a lot of innate intelligence," Bob said.

"What does that mean?" I asked.

"He's got the basic materials, but he will need the skills to be able to put those materials to use in a way that will result in a completely independent life, particularly when it comes to his social interaction."

"If we look at all the successful blind people in the world, the ones who seem to be really socially adjusted, they are in a very small, select group—maybe five percent of the total blind population," I explained. "Then there's another twenty-five percent of the blind adults who have a particular skill they can sell and that allows them to live independent lives, but they are uncomfortable in social terms. I call it a social glitch. Now I haven't had the chance to meet Jim yet, but I do know that's part of the developmental process and it's the kind of thing that parents really have to know about. You see, so many blind children seem to play on a different planet."

Bob laughed. "I've observed that."

"It's as if they are taking in information and processing it in different ways, and then it comes out on different levels of play that are very unique to them. One of the secrets for me," I said, "was to get sighted kids to play with me and enjoy being part of my world. So, Robin, what's your perception today? Who do you think Jim is?"

Looking back, the MH label was a cruel absurdity. I haven't observed signs of CP or seizures or any of the other ridiculously wrong labels that have been attached to him at one time or another. In fact, Jim doesn't exhibit many behaviors typical of blind children. I think he may even be a genius. Now that he's in with the regular-education kids, I can see a huge change, and I think the kids really like him. I am certain Jim will grow into a successful independent blind adult like you, Tom."

"You know, we've got a lot more to learn, and I hope you're right. But it still seems as if you're on separate paths. Bob, you seem to have taken a real defined realist approach to Jim. You have all of the parental hopes for his future, but I believe that you still think Robin is chasing windmills."

"It has always been that way," said Bob, "but I've learned to live with it. I try to stay focused on who Jim is, rather than who he might be. I tend to take a more practical look at him in relation to his peers and to life."

"I hate that phrase," Robin said. "The more practical look is an easier way to say a more limited look."

"Well, when was the last time he was invited to a sleep-over or when did he have kids over here to play?"

"Little girls love him. They play with him all the time," Robin said.

"Little girls aren't enough," Bob said, "but he is still young and I think this can all change."

"It can," I said.

Robin interrupted. "Boys are insensitive and rough. They don't give a darn if Jim gets hurt emotionally or physically."

"And that's just what Jim needs," Bob responded. "Boys bring out masculine traits. They'll teach Jim to be tough, and, hopefully, give him the drive and ambition to achieve and compete with them."

"I didn't get started socially until I met Billy Hannon," I said. "I know every child with a disability needs a Billy Hannon, just like I hope every parent coping with a child with a disability gets to know other parents who have children with disabilities who can help them along the way."

"One of the dangers," Robin said, "is that you can limit your friends to those who have children with disabilities only. We all have to really work at not doing that."

"I'm glad we covered this point," I said, "but I want to go back to what was going on in Jim's life—in the four-to-five-year-old period. I know you moved to a new house in a new district, and didn't you tell me that you had a real problem with bus service to take Jim to the Blind Children's Center?"

"It was hard," Robin said. "We had three different drivers before finding one who had a blind child herself and really understood how to handle Jim on the hour-and-a-half-long bus ride. They actually became good friends. It's funny how Jim becomes friends with people who extend to understand him. I wish that had been the case with all of his teachers, starting with his visually handicapped [VH] teacher in the new district. When I met her, she looked great. She drove a nice car, dressed well, and she told me that she not only taught VH, but that she also was credentialed to teach deaf and deaf/blind. Yet I checked later with her college, and her professor apologized because these were all just paper degrees with no training in the competencies needed to teach these populations. She was part of an experiment. She didn't know braille, sign, or hand spelling for deaf/blind. She knew no alternative means of communication. I will never understand how the California Department of Education managed to make such a serious mistake. Her story gets more serious as we go along.

"I had invited her to go with me to a conference sponsored by the Blind Children's Center. I even agreed to pay for her baby-sitter and drive with her to the conference. I was willing to do anything to help facilitate her teaching my son. I even found her a house nearby so that the educational process could go easier. Anyway, I finally talked her into coming to the conference, and you won't believe what happened!

"She was sitting next to me. All the medical doctors and special education professionals were sharing terrific ideas, and she said, 'Oh, darn, Robin, I forgot my knitting. I get so bored at these conferences.' I knew from that moment on I couldn't reach her.

"Then onto the conference stage walked an incredible woman, another one of the 'A' list people. Her name is Lois Harrell—actually in our house we call her 'Wonderful Lois.' I knew from the beginning that she was extraordinary. Nothing is status quo with Lois. She was talking about the concepts of closure and fragmentation in the blind child's world. She had a piece of string. 'Close your eyes, and pull that string through your fingers,' she said, 'and pretend that you've never seen anything in your life. Now tie a knot at each end of the string.' She wanted us to understand how much easier it was for the blind child to process the beginning and end of the string if there is a knot at each end rather than just have the string go through their fingers without it.

"Then she talked about showing a congenitally blind child an object. When you just hand the child an object and say, 'Okay, this is an apple, this is a chair, this is a desk,' what does she really know about the objects? You need to show her the beginning, the end, the top, and the bottom of the object. The child must see the whole object with her hands, so she'll get an idea of closure.

"Jim's world is a fragmented jigsaw puzzle, comprised of millions of pieces of unrelated information the size of his small hands. Often, blind children are trying to cope with closure and they don't really have a sense of how one object connects to another."

"I used to call it dimensional reference, Robin," I said. "I think Lois is really right. When a sighted person holds a round ball, he or she understands how the ball relates in space and what its uses are. But blind children only understand that the round ball, if they know round at all, is limited to what they hold in their hands. So closure is a tough concept. We really are fragmented."

"I'm glad you said that, Tom. I feel that with Jim all the time. When Lois finished her speech, I turned to the VH teacher. She said she didn't understand a word Lois said. But when I looked around the room, everyone else was filled with enthusiasm, and I knew I just had to get to know Lois Harrell. She was another one of those people who understood blindness intuitively, instinctively. That's what made her special. So I started to write to her and communicate with her.

"I'm so glad I did. Jim was almost five years old and was

going to make the change from preschool to elementary school. Thank God we were communicating with Lois. I was having the worst time trying to get Jim potty-trained. You know, Tom, you have to have a child potty-trained before you can send him to school, and I knew I needed the help of Wonderful Lois. I finally wrote, 'Look, Lois, could you come down and visit us? I'll buy your air tickets. Could you just give us a few days?' She agreed, and boy did I learn a lot."

"Bob, what did you think of Lois?"

"I think she's spectacular. She gave us both so much confidence."

Robin said, "When she came, she gave me one condition: she said that from the time she arrived it was going to be Lois and Jim. I could video them, I could take notes, I could observe, but it was Lois and Jim. When Lois stepped off that plane and I looked at her radiant face and knowing eyes, I knew that everything was going to be okay. She was going to help my Jim. She came to the house and said, 'Oh, Jim, you're still wearing your diapers. Take off your diaper, Jim, and throw it away.' And then he had to touch his wet diaper. And that started a change right away. When he was in underwear and had an accident, he had to wash his own clothes and that made him think about it. That was the first time I began to understand that you could take a hard line, or maybe I should say a hard, loving line, toward a blind child. A blind child needs appropriately high expectations, as does every child."

Bob said, "I remember Robin telling me that they made real egg salad sandwiches. They cracked the eggs with their hands so that Jim would know what the eggs felt like before you cooked them. And then they cooked them and peeled the shells. Then they got the bread out and put the egg on the bread, and it was all hands on. This was the same approach taken by the O.T. at Easter Seals and all of the special people who have affected Jim's life, and it is an incredibly successful approach."

Robin and Bob agreed about that point.

Robin said, "Let me give you another example. We were all having breakfast together the next morning. I handed Jim a piece of toast, and he said, 'Egg bread.'

"And I said, 'No, it's not egg bread.'

"And the way Jim said it, it sounded totally inappropriate, but Lois said, 'Wait a minute, that's not inappropriate, that *is* the egg bread.'

"And I said, 'No, it's not, Lois, it's toasted wheat bread.'

"'Yes,' Lois said, 'but that was the bread that we made egg salad sandwiches out of yesterday. Jim isn't inappropriate, he's indicating terrific perception.' And I thought, 'Just like the occupational therapist said, 'think of the donut, not the hole.'

"Throughout the rest of the time that Lois was with us, it was obvious that she was opening worlds of possibilities that I hadn't even considered. She kept applying a connection approach to perception from Jim's point of view. She kept quoting from Darwin's theory, that nothing purposeless perpetuates. With Jim this meant that I had to determine why he was behaving a certain way by looking at the world from his totally blind point of view. And that's not all she said. She regarded blind children as people whose individuality needs to be respected. She believed that every blind child is as much an individual as any sighted child. In fact, this is one of the isolating factors of blindness for parents. There are so many variables—like environment, medical etiology, degree of visual impairment—in such a small population, that parents have essentially no models to compare their child with to understand behavior or predict development. She also said that we have to respect the disability. Sight is the primary integrating sense, so that you have to respect the significance of its absence, and its impact on the development of this human being, without letting it become the dominant label. Initially, no incidental learning takes place with totally blind children."

"That's great advice," I said. "I've been a blind person for forty-six years, and I couldn't have said it better."

Robin said, "We fought major battles on a couple of levels. In education, we struggled with whether he was visually handicapped or multi-handicapped. We now know that he is not MH, but because the system labeled him that way, we faced this ongoing battle. Second, within visual handicaps, I believe that the totally blind child perceives life differently from the partially sighted child. I don't know when this is going to solve itself. This is just something we don't know much about."

"I agree," I said. "Most of the blind people I've met, even those who are extremely successful, differ in their perception of the world from others, but I think that's just fine. I call it a glitch. In the end, we're all trying to mainstream, to find a balanced place in society between who we are as individuals, and how we fit."

There was a pause.

"I don't know Jim yet, folks, but I'm sure of this: he is going to get to the place that's appropriate for him. Parents can only help their child reach that appropriate place. They can provide them with every advantage. They can be as aggressive as it is possible to be on behalf of the child they love. They can support every activity and development the child indicates he or she is interested in. They can drive the education system forward to get the best for their child, but in the end the child will find the appropriate place.

"So keep challenging the system, keep breaking down the barriers, but be willing to recognize, not compromise, Jim's social balance. Get him involved in neighborhood activities, but please understand who he is, and not who you want him to be."

There was another pause.

"Then what can we expect, Tom?" Bob said. "What can we expect for him?"

Robin cut in. "The expectations for blind people are too low, they're just too low. We don't know what we can expect from him yet."

"That's right," I said, "but these are good practical questions Bob is raising."

Robin said, "My primary objective is that Jim be independent, that he be a taxpayer, and never be dependent on anyone. Every year when we go to his I.E.P. meetings, I tell the team the same thing. They ask me what my goals are, and I always say, 'Make my son a taxpayer.' On every day of every year, I'm going to make sure that Jim gets the most from this system. I'm committed to that. It's my mission."

I could almost hear her breathing hard, and neither Bob nor I wanted to say anything to her.

"And I'll tell you something else," she said, "I'm going to make sure he learns to read braille. He's just now started, and is enjoying it. It's the best thing that ever happened to him. It's literacy for him, and a real key to independence and it proves he's VH, not MH. We're winning, Jim and I. We're winning."

"We're all winning," Bob said. "And we're all in this together."

I'm sure a look passed between them.

"I think that's all for today," I said. "Let's enjoy a great barbecue and we'll take up the question of Jim's education in the next session."

When we began our second day, Bob chose to work, while my parent commando, Robin, came to our home and took me through the twists and turns of Jim's education. I was once again struck by her competence and her commitment as we looked at her next battlefield.

"Robin, tell me about education for a blind child in California."

"Well, here's how it works. It's all wound up with money.

The entire state is carved into SELPA (Special Education Local Plan Area) regions. SELPAs aren't necessarily cut along county lines. They're determined according to population and their ability to provide all the needed special-education services. For instance, Los Angeles has a big population, so L.A. Unified School District is its own SELPA. Out where I live, the SELPA is made up of a number of smaller school districts, covering a lot of area. Now the theory behind all this was good. Basically in a big rural area like this, if you only have one braille-reading child, like Jim, you can still offer him the appropriate services somewhere in the SELPA.

"But you know about the best laid plans of mice and men. The SELPA is supposed to have a director to facilitate the delivery of services, and we pay him a lot of money for it. But every year, the SELPA director and representatives of the individual school districts within the planning area have what I like to think of as the "Special Education Poker Game," during which they dole out the state money to the districts. I'm convinced that there are trades going on all the time among the districts in terms of how and what Special-Needs-group requests get addressed that year.

"We couldn't get the help Jim needed in our SELPA, and Jim wasn't offered an interdistrict transfer to enter L.A. Unified. No one cared that the VH teacher in our district didn't know braille, much less how to teach it. As far as they were concerned, she had a VH credential, and that satisfied their legal obligation to us. Even though there were competent VH teachers in other districts in the SELPA, not one of these districts would accept Jim as a student. The SELPA director could not or would not help us. My understanding is that the purpose of the SELPA system is to solve problems like ours, yet it didn't help us in any way. To the parent, the SELPA system is a mystery.

"The first sign that I was going to have major bureaucratic

problems came when I was working to give Jim a mainstream preschool education closer to home than Blind Children's Center in L.A. We found a lovely preschool right near our home that was willing to take Jim. We figured we needed a preschool consultant from Braille Institute of Los Angeles County for Jim, so we asked Braille to come and help us. But because this preschool was one mile outside the L.A. County line, Braille Institute of Los Angeles said it couldn't help, and that we would have to go to the Braille Institute program in Santa Barbara. Santa Barbara was too far away, so they couldn't help us either. Imagine, we couldn't get the rules to bend for one mile. I don't want to put Braille down, it just gave me the first indication of what our future might be like."

"Systems and situations," I said. "They just never quite match up. Parents do scramble when they are trying to do the best they can. There is no clear-cut road in the system. You have to trust your instincts, and I suppose you got your first taste of battling the system when you went to Jim's first I.E.P."

"That's right, Tom. First, Jim was five years old and he was going to have his I.E.P. and we walked in prepared to do battle. I'd been dealing with the knitting VH teacher for the last couple of years, and I knew how incompetent she was to teach Jim. She arrived at the I.E.P. meeting with her boss, both dressed in white coats, like doctors. I couldn't believe it. It was kind of humorous really. Remember, she was legally certified but unqualified to be the itinerant VH teacher for the district.

"Tom, I need to tell you; I have been so involved in this issue over the years. Recently, I testified before the Special Education Division of the Department of Education, because they were trying to change the VH credential. These teachers get little enough training as it is. They only have one class in braille, and the State wanted to water down this credential even further by also training them to teach mentally handicapped children, within the same curriculum. This would exacerbate the situation for parents of blind children because there would be an even greater tendency to label blind children as mentally handicapped. Plus there would be even less training in VH competencies, like braille, than now, which is minimal enough. So when we testified, we were able to maintain at least the status quo.

"But back to the dreaded I.E.P. meeting. Bob had his lawyer briefcase with all the volumes of the Education Code and I had an agenda; I wanted to get Jim into the Frances Blend program in L.A. Unified School District, because I thought that was the best place for him."

"Tell me about Frances Blend, Robin."

"Remember, Tom, L.A. is a self-contained SELPA. Because its population is so big, it has all kinds of money. And because it has so many minorities, it also gets Chapter One help from the Federal Government. According to everyone I spoke to, Blend was the only day school for the blind anywhere in the country. Otherwise I would have to send my child away to a state blind school. Initially, the VH teacher told me that there would be no problem getting Jim into Blend. She called me back in May, just before the I.E.P. meeting, and told me to get a glass of wine and sit down. She said that the School District people were going to change their minds and that Jim couldn't go to Blend. She was going to be his teacher.

"I went berserk. I said to her, 'You're not qualified to teach Jim by your own admission!'

"And she said, 'Let me work with him, Robin. I think we can handle all of his problems right here in the district. Let me experiment with him. I know we can find ways to handle Jim's needs.'

"'My son is not going to become one of your experiments. You don't even know braille!' I said, and I hung up on her.

"This was such a bad time for our marriage. I wanted Bob

to be the knight in shining armor, to save the princess and her blind son, and slay the school district dragon. I even suggested that we move into a house within the boundaries of L.A. Unified. Bob became incensed. He had finally achieved his dream. He had his law office close to home, and he believed that life was terrific. All through the last five years he'd given up everything for blindness, and blindness wasn't going to take this away from him. I hated him for saying that. It was just a horrible time."

"Robin, did you find Bob's reaction selfish?"

"I probably did at the time, but I understand his point of view now. Bob doesn't like to go to the parent conferences, and he thinks that the fathers' group meetings are a waste of time. Now I don't know if this is denial or whether this is how he really feels, but he clearly lets me fight these wars and doesn't want to be involved in these kinds of situations. On the other hand, he's great at playing with Jim, and sharing with him. I know how much he loves Jim. It's just a different priority."

"So let's go back to the IEP. Who was in the room?"

"There was the VH teacher and her boss, but we didn't have the director of Special Education there. So I suppose we were in trouble right away because it became a middle management meeting. Bob and I went in there loaded with people, both of his parents, my dad, my friend Gerry, and then a great Parent Advocate, who was the mother of a blind child. I also brought several people from the Blind Children's Center."

"Robin, do you think you overwhelmed these people? Was it a fair fight?"

"Fair to whom, Tom? It's Jim's life we're talking about, his educational life, and ultimately his future. They weren't being fair to us. The district had all the people, power, and money. All we had was a five-year-old blind son in desperate need of a blind-appropriate education. Overwhelming these people with Jim's team was the whole point, and it was the only strategy available to us. We needed to show blindness was the primary handicapping condition, the VH teacher's lack of competency to address this handicap, and the lack of appropriate educational placement in the district. This was an adversarial situation unfortunately. They were not going to offer an appropriate educational setting for Jim outside the district with a qualified teacher unless they were forced into it. We were at Armageddon!

"Parents of blind children are at a great bargaining disadvantage with school districts, and there are no private schools for these children. They must use the public system. Add to this the extremely low incidence of total blindness. These children are spread very thinly across our huge country. Also the demand for qualified VH teachers far exceeds the supply, and even well-intentioned school districts have a difficult time hiring them. The SELPA system is supposed to provide a solution in California, but districts still have autonomy and often refuse to cooperate with each other for the benefit of a blind child. I've always tried to be accommodating, but sometimes I get to a place where I have to dig in. So I brought all the troops.

"We spent four and a half hours setting out goals and objectives that we purposely made very long and complicated, and then we got down to the nitty-gritty. Where was the right place for Jim to get an education? The VH teacher and her boss finally presented us with the classrooms they were prepared to offer Jim. And that's when we had the train wreck. Thank God Bob was there. He kept squeezing my hand under the table and telling me to calm down. We left that meeting completely unresolved, but to show good faith, over the next few days, we went through the exercises, and we looked at these classrooms, and they were totally inappropriate. The one in which they wanted most to place Jim had kids with aphasia, who had trouble speaking and were hard to understand. Speech was Jim's strongest area. Being in an aphasic class would have delayed him in an area in which he was ahead, not to mention severely limiting his ability to communicate with his classmates. This was one of the lowest points of my life. I just didn't know what to do, and time was running out. It was the middle of the summer, and Jim had to start school someplace in the fall. I was going from district to district in the SELPA trying to talk to people. I don't even know why I was doing that, because actually school districts should have been talking to school districts. It isn't the responsibility of a parent, but that's the way it works."

"You weren't getting any professional help?" I asked.

"That's absolutely right. Parents are told that the school districts will operate in these cases as your advocate, finding the best possible educational setting for your child, but it doesn't work that way. What I wanted was an interdistrict transfer to get Jim into Blend, but nobody really cared enough to help us carry the case forward. We got crazy. We even put our house up for sale, which almost cost us our marriage because Bob didn't want any part of this. But I knew we had to do something for Jim. I was thinking we'd move to Simi Valley, where I'd heard there was a good teacher. Simi is in our own SELPA. Even so, we couldn't get an interdistrict transfer just to Simi— 15 minutes away—so Jim could have a teacher who knew braille.

"Finally we decided to move to L.A., where there was a complete program and not just one good teacher. I realized the impossibility of cutting across district lines; nobody helps.

"I had one hope, just one hope: I appealed to the principal at Blend. She also heads all of the VH services for L.A. Unified

School District. I felt that she really could make it happen if she wanted to. So this time we didn't put on our lawyers' suits, we put on our beggars' hats. I told her that I'd do anything, from raising money to cleaning toilets. But she had too many children in her program that year, and it was hard for her to make room for Jim. Since then, I've come to understand the difficult decisions she has to make as an administrator of such a large program. But at the time I was devastated. At this point, we had less than two weeks to go before the kids went back to school, and Jim still didn't have a school to attend.

"I decided 'I'm going to become legal.' So I looked into the California Education Code and found two helpful sections giving a district discretionary grounds to permit interdistrict transfers. The problem was they were discretionary with the receiving district, but I thought maybe I had a chance. One code section said that if a parent is employed in a school district, the district may take the child. The second said that if child care is provided in that school district, the district may take the child. So Bob's mother signed up to do child care for me right away. I even went further than that. I found a job with a lawyer in L.A. who specialized in representing families of children with disabilities in their battles against school districts and other public agencies. She made several calls to L.A. Unified in our behalf. But because the code sections were discretionary with the receiving district, we were still denied an interdistrict transfer.

"Then I decided that the best thing Bob and I could do was to buy a condominium in L.A. I'd live there with the kids during the week, and we'd be husband and wife during the weekend. What a crazy solution. In the end, we didn't do that because our marriage would not have survived."

"But you still have your discretionary education codes?" I said.

"That's right. And I started to write letters to everybody,

trying to make something happen, but the clock was running. And we were losing. At one point, we were referred to the district offices of L.A. Unified School District. I was down there at the district office with Jim. He had his tape recorder on and was singing along with all of those patriotic songs from the album 'Wee Sing America.' Now there I was in the richest state in the United States, I had paid my taxes, and all I wanted was to have my blind child, who needed specialized help, transferred to a different school district where there were qualified teachers, and I was getting stonewalled at every turn. I just couldn't make it happen. Parents don't win every battle in the war, and my blind son, who had so far to go with so much to learn, was sitting in the school district offices of the second largest school district in the United States and no one gave a darn whether he received an education or not.

"In the interdistrict transfer office of L.A.U.S.D., the head clerk told me, 'You'll never get a transfer. Only regular-education kids are getting transfers. We've been told not to give transfers to Special Ed students.' I wrote down her name, the date, and exactly what she said. Then I called the Office of Civil Rights, and an attorney there said it sounded like a good discrimination case. He sent me forms to complete, but about this time I changed my strategy. It occurred to me I could spend the rest of my life fighting the educational bureaucracy in court, in the media, in Sacramento, and every other public arena. But while I was doing this, Jim would be getting older. And he wouldn't be in a satisfactory education setting. So although I might ultimately win the war, I'd lose the biggest battle. I'd lose my own son. Jim and I were pawns in a big chess game where the king, queen, knights, and all the players with the big moves were in the education establishment.

"I decided the only way to get my son the education he needed was to play the game by the rules that had already been set. At one point, the principal at Blend said, 'Why don't you put Jim into the California State School for the Blind in Northern California. They do a good job.'"

Now the anger had turned to tears and we waited again.

"And that seemed to be the only alternative?" I said.

"Yes," she said.

"So what did you do?"

"I called Lois, and she was the first person to tell me that maybe the principal was right. Maybe this was the only alternative available at this time. She said we have to respect that blindness is different. There are so few blind children and so many of them have been mislabeled developmentally delayed and multi-handicapped. Blind children need the opportunity for education in a setting where blindness is understood and their specific unique needs are recognized and addressed, especially during critical window periods of learning. A school for the blind perhaps could offer Jim the best program. Then I had several long conversations with a friend whose son was up at CSB at the time. Parent-to-parent networking is very important. She convinced me that CSB was a safe place for Jim to receive an excellent blind-specific education. The fact is, when you're going to send your little boy away from home, there is no best situation."

"I agree with you, Robin," I said. "I went away to a school for the blind when I was five, and it was hard on everybody. I'm sure it was hardest on my mother. So is that what you decided to do?"

"We did, Tom. We didn't have very much choice. When we first went up to look at CSB, Bob was prepared not to let Jim go away to school. But Lois met us, and we saw the classroom Jim was going to be in. It was so hard, because we were forced to make immediate decisions based on the circumstances we found ourselves in. We also met the supervisor of the Young

Children's Dorm. You know how you can look at someone and know right away that they're terrific? That's how we felt about her."

"Robin, this doesn't seem quite in balance to me, because you've now told me that on this day, she was an 'A' list person and you were with Lois, who was an 'A' list person. And I understand that because these people were terrific, you felt steam-rolled into saying yes, so it's hard for me to grasp what was wrong."

"Let me tell you the rest of my story, then maybe you'll understand. First of all, your mother has probably told you how difficult it was when she sent you off to Perkins when you were five. There's no way to describe this level of pain. It is emotionally devastating to send your little boy off to a residential school, even though it was the best, and only, alternative at the time. I simply never will get over the guilt I feel about all that."

"Neither will my mother," I said. "That's the one constant she refers to when I ask her about my childhood—her guilt about sending me to boarding school. Robin, did Jim come home just on holidays, or once a month, or what?"

"It was very difficult. We flew him back and forth every week. I asked the school to get him to the airport on Fridays, and to pick him up on Sunday nights. They did a wonderful job and never missed a flight in over two years. I used to call again and again to make sure that people were doing their jobs. I even contacted pediatricians up there and had a standing Saturday appointment with our own doctor at home to make sure that Jim's ears were checked. I feared flying all the time would hurt his ears, especially with his history of infections. You know, a blind person's principal sense is hearing. And every week my stomach would be in knots. I would call the dorm at three and four in the morning if it was a cold night in Thousand Oaks, just to make sure they had plenty of blankets on him. I tried to mother him from four hundred miles away. Fortunately, the dorm staff was excellent, and did a terrific job of caring for the kids and teaching them daily living skills. There's a horrible price parents sometimes pay for loving their children and thinking that they have to do what they perceive to be the right thing."

"Robin, I guess we're back to that business again, of instinct and perception; I'm learning that parents really are on the horns of a dilemma. Was there anything you could do to ease your pain?"

"Yeah, Tom, get involved. And that's what I did. I became the President of the Parent Association. Now here I was living in Southern California, and over the course of the years, I started driving all the way up to Northern California and staying for probably one week a month at a motel near the school or the parent apartment on campus, so that I could be involved as a parent."

"Wow, what a sacrifice," I said.

"Oh no, not a sacrifice," Robin said. "Responsibility, and love."

"Okay, within that responsibility, tell me how you felt about the California State School for the Blind."

"I absolutely loved most of the people I knew there. They're great people, and they really are committed. My problems had to do with educational philosophy, and with some of the decisions made about Jim. But I want to be real clear; there were some real 'A' people there. So let me explain. Did you see the movie *Children of a Lesser God*?"

"I loved it," I said.

"Well, that was a little like CSB. You know the scene where the headmaster said to William Hurt, 'Nobody's trying to change the world around here. Just trying to help a few deaf kids get along a little better, that's all. Everything else is razzle-dazzle'?"

We both laughed.

"I believe expectations for Jim and the other students were too low, and there wasn't much of an attempt to bring the younger students in contact with regular-education students in the area. Now into this environment are thrown Jim Rosso, and his mom with many high expectations. He's a very strong-willed kid. And the fact that I was fighting all these battles and that he was away from home at such a young age may have caused some emotional scarring for him, so that his educational issues probably became mixed with emotional ones. But he went to this school, and because their expectations weren't high enough for him, I have to say he took advantage of it. And, by doing that, he got categorized."

"Explain that," I said.

"Well, he was in class with his first teacher and there was an age span in this class of about five years, so kids were being taught on different levels. But because the principal had talked to Lois, Jim was put in an academic VH room, which was where I wanted him to be. So how did he handle it? Jim blew it, big time. He started by trailing along the wall and pulling all the posters off. And then he did what a lot of kids do. He challenged the teacher. He said, 'What are you gonna do if I throw this braille writer on the floor?'

"'Well,' she said, 'we'll take it to the library and then you won't have it.' Which was just what Jim wanted, so what did he do? Threw it on the floor as hard as he could. Right away he was in a conflict with the VH teacher.

"From then on, it was downhill. This was a major battle I lost. In Jim's second year, he got demoted to a non-academic, predominantly MH class. Throughout the year, they had fun and took lots of field trips. The teacher was great, the kids loved him. If you asked Jim today, he'd say he was one of his favorite teachers, but Jim wasn't working. I kept trying to get them to change him back into the first class and start teaching him braille. I knew he was ready to learn it. During one of the most amazing days I ever spent up there, Jim was in the non-academic class, but he could hear the other kids next door spelling. He could spell more of the words than any of the members of that class. I told the principal about Jim's spelling.

"He said, 'Yes, I know he spells well. He learned phonics by listening through the accordion door to the teacher next door.' And I committed myself that day to moving him back into her class, but she didn't feel he belonged there because he was too immature, so I never succeeded."

"Actually, you took him out of CSB the next year, right?"

"I did. Like everything in life, there was an incident that made me realize I had to become more actively involved and bring him home. Remember the earthquake in San Francisco? It was awful. For hours I didn't know what had happened, whether Jim was all right, because the phone lines were tied up. CSB is new and earthquake proof, so it's the safest place to be in a quake. But I didn't know if Jim was there or on a field trip. And I still had questions about braille. There wasn't a younger VH class where the kids were at Jim's educational level. Also, after two years, I was getting tired of dividing my life between Northern and Southern California, and the impact this was having on my family. Lindsey often had to come home to an empty house, and Bob to an empty bed. Most of our weekend family time was spent at the airport meeting Jim's planes. It just seemed to me that I'd have to take another stab at working with L.A. Unified School District.

"The final straw came with Jim's assessment. First of all, I think most psychologists along with nearly every social worker I've ever known are full of baloney. That's how I felt about this Assessment Team. It was an independent team and it got state funding to assess blind children. Picture this, Tom. Instead of observing Jim on a daily basis at the school and in his dorm, they moved him into a strange place, the parent apartment, with me, to conduct the assessment. That's absurd. How can you put a blind child in an unfamiliar, one-room setting with his mom for a week, and do a valid assessment? They tested his daily living skills in the apartment and timed him on how long he took to get ready for school. But he didn't know his way around the apartment and we had no routine, so he wasn't very impressive. If they had observed him in his own dorm room or spoken with his terrific dorm supervisor, they would have realized he was very competent. The dorm staff was great and should have been consulted much more. It was crazy!

"Along with that, they took him in the daytime to their office and gave him developmental tests. I argued with them about these tests and the results. For instance, they wanted to see if Jim understood the concepts of same and different, so they showed him two spoons with different handles. They wanted him to answer that the spoons were the same, but they weren't to him because of their handles. Jim's whole world is based on distinguishing tiny nuances. He can pick up any of his audio tapes and tell exactly which one it is, even though there's no braille label or anything to distinguish it from another tape as far as a sighted person is concerned. Somehow Jim knows one unmarked tape from another by feel. You can't fool him. [This will be a great party trick when he gets older.]

"The assessment team didn't understand this, and when I tried to explain it to one of the testers, she said, 'Don't do this to me, Robin, or I won't let you watch the testing.' I phoned Lois and she tried to intervene on Jim's behalf, by telling them about all of Jim's skills. But they said since he demonstrated these skills with Lois and not with them, they credited Lois's teaching ability rather than Jim's learning ability. And these testing issues continue.

"Recently another psychologist tested Jim because it was time for the required three-year assessment. She asked him to define the word 'island.' He's been to Hawaii, and responded, 'warm beaches.' He got the answer wrong because he was supposed to say, 'land surrounded by water'—a visual definition. Psychologists fail to take into account the blind viewpoint, as well as the limited information a blind child has acquired in the early years when his understanding of the world is so piecemeal. You have to give a blind child plenty of time to put it all together. The principal at CSB says age nine seems to be the magical year when things come together cognitively for blind kids—and that's how it was for Jim. Some kids may be able to handle a week of such intensive testing, but Jim couldn't. He refused to participate in many of the tests, or even to converse with the team on their terms. They decided that he was obsessive-compulsive. How can you think of a blind six-year-old as obsessive-compulsive!? He doesn't know enough about the world outside his own dimension space to be obsessive-compulsive. He was stressed out from all the tests, and I think he knew the team didn't believe in him or expect much from him. He knew they weren't trying to see things from his blind point of view, and he was right.

"By this time I was getting used to the crazy labels people put on Jim. Obsessive-compulsive was just another one. When he didn't walk on time, they told me he had an orthopedic problem and they wanted to put on knee braces. When he didn't potty-train on time, they told me he had a renal or bladder problem. When he got excited and his hands shook, they told me he was either having a seizure or maybe had CP. When he was rocking, like Ray Charles, they told me he might be autistic. All these labels were given by professionals who just didn't know enough about congenitally blind children. So when they said obsessive-compulsive, I didn't believe it, and I didn't want him to stay in an educational setting where he might be viewed this way.

"Now it's clear that Jim is 'just blind,' and he's viewed this way in his present educational setting, so the story had a happy ending. I remember the first time I heard the phrase 'just blind.' 'Just blind,' isn't that enough? I thought at the time. And really, it is."

"But you had a hell of a problem," I said. "All these professionals had been labeling Jim as MH, but you thought he was VH."

"No, no. I *know* he's VH."

"I'm sorry, Robin, I know he's VH, too. But when you brought him home, you had to figure out where to put him in the system again."

"Yes, in order to get him into Frances Blend, he had to reside within the physical parameters of L.A. Unified School District. So we put him in the dorms at a private placement facility because we all felt he needed to be closer to home. And then, once I got him in Blend, I had to convince the Blend people that he was VH."

"What a confusing period of time this turned out to be. It must have been very painful for all of you."

"Tom, I have to share something with you. I've been trying to decide whether I should for the last few days. When Jim was at the private facility in L.A . . ."

Robin was choking now, the tears were coming, and I didn't know what was bothering her so I just hugged her, and we waited.

She continued. "There was a staff person in the dorm who was there only a short time. Jim told us that this person touched him, and told him to relax, and then when Jim wouldn't relax, he hit him in the stomach. I don't know that it was sexual, I just know that Jim said that he was touched by this person. I feel so guilty about having put him in a place away from home again. The first thing parents think about when they have to place their children in residential settings is the issue of inappropriate touching both by the adults in charge and by other children. It's a valid concern. At CSB Jim was absolutely safe. But in other settings, it's important for parents to look at the physical layout of the rooms, the amount of staff supervision, even the pay scale of dorm staff, and the thoroughness of background checking done before someone is hired. These insure a safe environment with high quality people. But there are no guarantees, and you can only do your best to evaluate the situation."

Now Robin was crying. I found myself thinking about all the pain that every parent who has a child with a disability must feel as they try desperately to figure out how to give their children the best possible opportunities to succeed, and then I cried, too.

As Robin settled down, she said, "Residential programs are an important option that should be available to blind children. CSB offers students like Jim a blind-specific education when their home districts fail to do so. For some students with dysfunctional homes, a caring dorm staff is far better than the adult supervision they get at home. For younger children, of course, the best situation is a loving family in a school district that provides an appropriate education. But unfortunately sometimes this just isn't available. I don't want other parents to start worrying, but I do want to say that the more often a parent can keep hands-on participation with their children and not send them away, the better off the child will be, and the better off the parent will be."

"I agree with you," I said. "So what did you do next?"

"Well, now I had to start the campaign at Blend to get Jim back into an academic VH classroom. While he was there, I volunteered for everything. I got to know the principal, and finally I was in her office one day and I tried to tell her that Jim wasn't MH, that he was VH. She started looking through Jim's file, and said, 'Robin, there isn't anything in this file that indicates that Jim is MH.'

"'That's right, because he's not,' I said. But, he still didn't have the 'ticket out' of MH. The ticket out is braille.

"So I found a special teacher at Blend. From this teacher I learned that programs themselves aren't all that important. The teacher is the significant factor—the teacher *is* the program. I talked her into teaching Jim braille on the side. He loved it! He flourished with it. That's the way he not only got out of MH, but how he got into the program he's in now—in a regular elementary school. Actually, he returned to our home district and got into a small special day class because of the excellent new VH teacher we now have in our district. What a tremendous person she is. And she went all over the place to find him just the right setting.

"He's getting along with the kids wonderfully, and every time I go to his school he's got a smile on his face. I know there will still be problems, but it's so much better now. I think there's a chance that Jim can become all the things that are possible for him. We're finally seeing the bright side of the moon. And I love it, Tom, I just love the feeling that there's a future. Everything's better for us now. Our marriage, our home. I'm still fighting battles, but at least I feel like there are solutions."

We both breathed a sigh of relief. This had been an incredible day. I was sitting across from this woman, whom I knew had never compromised on her own beliefs about her son. She had learned to use the system, and her single-minded focus on where Jim was going to go was absolute. And I know she had enough support to get there, with Bob and Lindsey and the friends I'd met. Robin will succeed on Jim's behalf. She now also has the support of Jim's wonderful new teachers: his VH teacher, orientation and mobility instructor, and classroom teacher.

Jim is now in a class, in a normal school, learning normal subjects. He sings in a community boys' choir, takes drum and karate lessons, and ballroom dancing. His classmates phone him during the week, and cheer him on in the school talent show, spring sing, and winter holiday program. He played the Wizard of Oz in the school play, and went to winter camp with his Sunday school class.

Maybe Jim's great VH teacher will leave the area; maybe Jim will land in a class where kids won't be sensitive toward him; maybe the Rossos will continue to struggle with the dreaded I.E.P.s; but there is hope on the horizon and the future is looking bright. I know how great Robin feels about all of this. She has earned the right to feel that good. She has fought every battle, and she has won them.

I want to close this chapter with a grocery list of the jobs that Robin has held in the blind community during Jim's early years. It clarifies the astounding commitment of my special friend.

- California Association of Parents of the Visually Impaired (CAPVI): Legislative Analyst, one year. Secretary, four years. Southern California contact parent, seven years.

- National Association of Parents of the Visually Impaired (NAPVI): member, nine years.

- Joint Action Committee of Organizations of and Serving the Visually Handicapped (JAC): Donation Chairman, Annual JAC Musical, two years.

- California Transcribers and Educators of the Visually Handicapped (CTEVH): Presenter CTEVH, Annual Statewide Conference, two years; parent member, nine years.

- Association for the Education and Rehabilitation of the Blind and Visually Handicapped (AER): parent member, eight years.

- Presenter, testimony before State Special Education Commission on Teacher Credentialing Changes proposed by the Commission for Teacher Credentialing: one year.

- Presenter, State Compliance Review Committee Hearing: three years.

- Ventura College Braille class, driver: two years.

- Retinitis Pigmentosa International, Ventura County Chapter: member, three years; driver, one year.

- California School for the Blind, Fremont: Parent Advisory Council President, two years. Parent Representative, Task Force for Dorm Reorganization, one year. Southern California contact parent, two years.

- Northern California Blind Olympics: parent volunteer, one year.

- Children's Vision Center, U.C. Davis: parent volunteer.

- Blind Babies Foundation Newsletter: parent contributor.

- Foundation for the Junior Blind, Los Angeles: Parent Advisory Council President, one year.

- Frances Blend School for the Visually Impaired, Los Angeles: Community Advisory Council Chairman, one year; Co-Chairman, one year. School Leadership Council Secretary, two years. Co-Chairman, Parent Orientation Tea, one year. Member, Committees on Budget, Equipment, School Discipline and Van Ness Interaction, two years. Library Assistant, one year; room mother, two years.

- Los Angeles Unified School District Advisory Council Representative: two years.

- Conejo Valley Unified School District, SELPA representative alternate, two years; SEDAC (Special Education District Advisory Committee), Meadows School Representative, two years.

CHAPTER

Diana

I COULD NOT POSSIBLY have written this book without dealing with the ultimate disability, the specter of death. Millions of parents every year face the loss, or at best, the survival of their children in a struggle where often the only weapons available are love and hope.

Diana Thomas is a single mother of four boys, living just outside Austin, Texas. It is tough enough to raise four young men between the ages of nine and seventeen, but if your oldest suffers a lengthy battle with leukemia, your life can only be described as complicated. Against all this, Diana has maintained an incredible relationship with her sons and has achieved re-markable professional success, considering the extremely diffi-cult odds. I interviewed her while she was visiting her parents in Southern California, and then in subsequent lengthy telephone conversations from her home in Texas.

"Tell me about your life after you got married," I asked.

"You know, Tom, maybe I was naive, but I figured we'd have a life like any couple."

"What do you mean?" I said.

"Well, family. The picket fence, a house in the suburbs. But Mike didn't want children."

"You mean, you didn't talk about this before marriage?"

"We did, but I figured I could change him. I was sure that after we had lived together for a while, he would want children, but he didn't. And he was very, very adamant about this. When we argued about it, he said, 'I don't want children *ever*. That's a closed issue.' But I developed lumps in my breast, and I believed birth control pills were the cause. The doctors assured me that they were not, but it's what I believed, so I stopped using the pill. I don't know . . . maybe I was involved in some sort of denial, maybe I was trying to drive my need for family through at any cost.

"I can remember telling Mike I was pregnant as if it were yesterday. He'd been away on a trip. When he came home he shared how much he'd missed me, so we went out to dinner. I thought it would be an incredibly romantic moment, so in the middle of dinner, I said to him, 'I'm pregnant.'

"Right off the top he said, 'I don't want this baby, and if you decide to have this baby, it's either the baby or me.' No conversation, no discussion. Simply, the baby or me.

"I even went to see my doctor about having an abortion. At that time, abortion was still illegal. I said to the doctor, 'My life is miserable, and I don't know what to do.'

"I'll never forget his reply. He said, 'You know, Diana, you have to live with only one person. Husbands can come and go, but the one human being you have to love is yourself. Do what's right for you. I'll do anything you want. If you want an abortion, I'll make sure you have it, and it's done correctly. But most of all, you have to do the right thing for you.'

"And so that decision was made, and I had to live with it. At that point, I couldn't envision leaving Mike, going away, or even going home to my folks pregnant. So I just stayed. I remember we had gone to a christening for another child on a Sunday and on the way home, in the car, he said to me, 'When is it going to be born?'

"I said, 'Soon; I hope this week.'

"The emotional pain was unbearable. It was far more difficult than any pain I have had since, during the delivery of any of my sons. When Jason was born on the next Wednesday, and Mike was out in the waiting area, after all that he had put me through, I could hear him yell, 'I've got a son, I've got a son.' He absolutely adored this child from the moment he laid eyes on him.

"Tom, I know this doesn't seem like part of the story you are trying to tell, but I want you to understand where we were coming from so that the intensity of what happened later is clear."

"As difficult as your pregnancy had been, was the time after Jason's birth good in the marriage?"

"In every marriage there are good times, and I suppose this was one for us. It's hard to remember now, after all the pain. But yes, this was a very good time for us.

"A year went by," she continued, "and even though Mike was beginning to succeed, I had to go back to work. I had worked in the Promotion Department of a big insurance company in Dallas. One of the people who had sold incentive gift items to the insurance company was a sharp, beautiful woman. She had said to me, 'If you ever want to get into sales, let me know.' Well, I guess I was ready. I got started in the incentive business with her company, and worked there for a year.

"Soon I realized that I was pretty good at sales, and figured maybe I could do just as well on my own. So I started Thomas Promotions when Jason was about two. During this time, there was another pregnancy, and I lost the baby. So that's why there was a three-and-a-half-year gap between Jason and Grant."

"You say that as though Mike agreed that you should be having babies. He didn't actually, did he?"

"No, he didn't. And when we had Grant, it was altogether different. Mike was happy Grant had been born, but, in retrospect, I can't say we were happy as husband and wife."

"Tell me about Grant, Diana."

"Grant is a special button. He's from the Gill side of the family. He's sensitive and brilliant, and though I think I give all my children the same amount of affection, I'm sure I focused on Grant. But Jason was a hard act to follow."

"What kind of a baby was Jason?" I asked.

"He was gorgeous, and he was a good baby. Right from the beginning, he was such an easy kid. Now that he's seventeen, I'm going through the toughest time in my life with him, but when he was a baby, he was perfect."

"Let me get a time sense, Diana. Grant was born three and a half years after Jason, so we're actually getting close to crunch time, aren't we?"

"We are. Jason's diagnosis came pretty soon. But at this point, I was doing tremendously well professionally. We'd bought a new house and I'd had a lot to do with contributing to it. I was very proud of what I was achieving, so Jason's sickness, in every sense, was an unbelievable shock. You know, at that point, Mike was actually proud of me, too. He loved to tell his friends that his wife had her own company in downtown Dallas, with eight salespeople working for her. I was on top of the world. Grant and Jason were in day care next to my office. I could see them at lunch. And we were really rolling. I didn't expect any crisis in our lives at the time."

"Well, I suppose we have to start talking about crisis," I said. "Tell me how it began."

"Grant was about eight months old and Jason was about

four, and we'd come out to California to visit my folks. When we would go to the beach, Jason complained that his ankles were hurting all the time. So I would rub his legs to try and ease the pain, but it never went away. Doctors have told me subsequently that it couldn't have had anything to do with leukemia, but I'm sure it did. By November of that year, he was having constant colds, and I took care of them as well as I could. I took him to the doctor, and we had strep tests and everything. But nobody saw any signs at all."

"What about you, Diana, what did you think?"

"I just couldn't get past the idea that the pain in his legs had to be more than the doctors were indicating. I'd get him dressed in the morning, and help him put his jeans on. He'd actually cry out, 'My ankles hurt!' I thought it was odd, but nobody would listen. He was my first child, so I didn't get overly alarmed. I thought it might be his growth plates or something. I tried to believe the professionals, so I kept him in school. Everything seemed to be okay until we got to December. He had a dreadful cold and felt rotten. It got to be close to Christmas time, and I remember thinking that he had had this cold forever. To cheer him up, I took him to a Christmas movie. We had to walk up a ramp to get to the theater, but he could hardly make it because his legs hurt so much. I carried him. That, in combination with the cold, made me take him back to the pediatrician. I didn't want him to feel bad for Christmas.

"Our regular doctor was on vacation so I saw a different doctor. I told her, 'He just feels awful.' She checked him. He had swollen glands, so she prescribed medication treating him for what she thought was strep. She was sure he would be all right in a week or so.

"I did everything I was supposed to do, but still he didn't feel better. A week later, I took him back. Now it was just before Christmas, and my own doctor had returned.

"We walked into the office. Jason was telling me about all

the things he wanted for Christmas, particularly a train that he could sit on and peddle around a little track. That was his big present. This was our first Christmas with him old enough to understand that Santa Claus was coming. It was a happy time and I was really excited. I got Jason up on the little examination table, and he took his shirt off.

"Dr. Levies came in and took one look at Jason, and I knew immediately something was very wrong. There was horror in his eyes. Not only had Jason's glands not shrunken, they had swelled by two hundred percent since the week before. By now, his stomach was distended because his liver was enlarged. The fact that it hadn't been detected earlier is just incomprehensible to me, because it had to have been enlarged the week before. I didn't notice it because I'm with Jason every day. But you would think a doctor would have seen it.

"As Dr. Levies looked at Jason's abdomen and palpated the area, I became alarmed. He said to me, 'I'm going to send you downstairs,' and he coughed a lot, the way people do when they're awkward. He didn't make eye contact with me but kept coming in and out of the office, as if he knew something but didn't have the capacity to tell me what it was.

"I had a great relationship with Dr. Levies and could feel the panic start to bubble up in my stomach. He finally said, 'I want you to get a blood test. I think Jason has mono.' In retrospect, I know he didn't actually believe Jason had mono. But until he was sure about the diagnosis, he didn't want to tell me anything. I'm sorry, Tom, I'm getting chills just sitting here talking about it."

That is not all that is happening, I thought. She's crying. There's a lot of that in this book. So we waited.

"What were you thinking right then?" I asked.

"I did what all parents do. I tried to cling to hope. I didn't know what was wrong, but my instincts said it was severe.

So when Dr. Levies told me that Jason had mono, I tried to believe it.

"After the lab drew the blood, we got in the car to drive home. I had an errand to run on the way. I completed the errand, but as I looked at Jason a nagging thought kept coming into my mind. Right around that time there was a lot of publicity about Chad Green, a little boy who had leukemia. His parents wanted him to have Laetrile—a drug that was being used in Mexico. They had moved him from the hospital and taken him to Mexico. There were many lawsuits to get him back to this country; the doctors were up in arms, feeling that the Greens had violated their medical prerogative. As I was driving, Chad Green kept popping into my mind, and I had no idea why. I remember thinking, 'Oh my God, I hope this isn't the same as Chad Green.' Is it fear, or real parent instinct? I don't know.

"We got home and I pulled the car into the garage. Mike's car was in the driveway. That was odd because Mike was supposed to be at work. When I walked into the house, Mike began acting strangely. He said, 'Why don't you put Jason down for a rest. I need to talk with you.' I knew then that something was bad.

"I put Jason to bed and came back into our room, and Mike said, 'Dr. Levies called. He wants us to take Jason straight to Children's Hospital because he has leukemia.'

"I fell to the floor; I actually fainted. I guess it wasn't as much a surprise to me as an affirmation of my worst fears. Mike had called my best friend to be there if I needed help. He never could face these kinds of problems with me. It probably was a precursor to the failure of our marriage. But to be fair to Mike, at a moment like this—actually at all of the moments of emotion or intimacy in our relationship—he just didn't know how to be involved. I suppose a lot of men are like that, and I can't hold him responsible for not being someone he isn't.

"It was amazing that we had to deal with the issue immediately; there was no preparation. We found out subsequently that Jason's leukemia was in such an advanced state—his white count was so out of control—that the doctors had to do something right away. They attacked the leukemia with every invasive form of chemotherapy available."

"Diana, were you dealing with life and death, or were you numb at this point?"

"Oh, I was very much thinking of death, because all I knew about leukemia at the time was that children died of it. Later I learned so much about the disease, but right then I thought that Jason was going to die. When you don't have knowledge, but you have fear, it is a horrible time.

"We got to Children's, and without any preamble or explanation, the doctors took Jason to do a bone marrow. I remember crying and thinking, 'I'll never see him again,' because I believed that he could die right then. I was trying to draw a picture of his face that would stay in my mind. I wanted to hold on to that face, and I wanted to hold on to my child, but I had to let the professionals do their job.

"Eventually, the doctor called us into her office. I had never met her before. She was a large, imposing woman who obviously had done this a lot. She looked at us and said, 'This is the worst part of my job. It's the moment I hate the most, because I have to tell you that your son does have leukemia. We have tested his marrow and we found that the disease is out of control.' Then she began to reel off words and statistics that went right over my head. Nothing meant anything, because I'd heard the word *leukemia*, and now it was reconfirmed. She said that his count was extremely high, and that it was critical he receive chemotherapy immediately. The doctors needed to control his immature white count."

"Diana, what do you mean when you talk about immature white count?"

"For most people, a normal white count is approximately 10,000, but in Jason's case, the immature, or new, cells' white count had almost taken over, meaning he had no immunity. He could have died of that cold. It isn't always leukemia that kills you; it's the ancillary infections that evolve out of the leukemia as the white cells explode.

"Leukemia is a type of cancer. The disease takes different forms. Jason had the most common variety, ALL [acute lymphocytic leukemia], which has the best track record for successful treatment. However, the professionals did point out to us that the success ratio wasn't very high—maybe twenty to thirty percent. Thank God, over the last ten years, some of the alternative breakthroughs, in the form of applied chemotherapy, have increased Jason's chances for survival.

"Another thing that really bothered us was that the mortality rate among boys was much higher than that of girls. We also needed to understand that Jason's leukemia was at a very explosive period. The doctor told us that she was going to start him immediately on a complex protocol. That phrase sounds so technical when you're talking about life and death. As I sat in a daze half listening to the doctor, I remember thinking that I was never going to let Jason live a day of his life burdened with the pain I was feeling. 'He's just a little boy,' I thought. 'He's waiting right outside for us, having just gone through his first painful bone marrow. I can't go to him and shake my head and cry and wail. I have to be lovingly strong.'

"Thank God he was as sick as he was, because he didn't ask any questions. I just told him he was going to check into the hospital. And we began a ten-day watch. They started to give him transfusions to get his white count up because, you see, there are good white cells and bad white cells, and the immature white are damaging. So by transfusion they were trying to raise the good white count since those cells fight infection. Then, in a couple of days, they began platelet transfusions. They were afraid he could bleed internally and the platelets would support the formation of good blood. Jason had no resistance for anything. In fact, he developed a staph infection in the area where they were giving the transfusion. He could have died from that infection."

"Diana, did the hospital allow you to stay in the room with Jason?"

"We could stay there, Tom, but at that time parents weren't provided any creature comforts.

"On December 23, my parents came for the holidays. The doctors said that even though Jason was an extremely sick little boy, they would let us take him home. So we did. On Christmas morning, Jason spiked a high fever. I couldn't even get him interested in his little train that went around the track. Nothing could touch him; nothing would interest him. He was that sick.

"We had to bring him back to the hospital. This time, the watch went on for a couple of weeks. We stayed in his room, sleeping in chairs, and we didn't take shifts. We were both involved. They put him back on chemo, there were more transfusions, and we just waited.

"In the middle of all of this, my mother got sick. She had heart palpitations, and she checked into the hospital just across the street from where Jason was. I remember running back and forth, checking on both of them. I don't know how people survive this kind of tension, but we did.

"We also started to get calls from our friends. People were shocked. They sent cards and gifts. But still, I never felt so distant from other human beings, even though they were supporting us. I knew they couldn't do a damn thing to help us.

"It's astounding how time stands still. Days and nights don't matter; hours, minutes, seconds don't matter. We lived within the four walls of our son's room. The doctors give him transfusions and chemo protocols, and we sit. They bring him back. We look at his face, and we see him losing ground, and we can't do anything about it, and we sit. Time is frozen. Days go by, and we sit.

"Then we really got jolted, because the doctors started cranial radiation along with the chemo. They don't do that anymore, but then they believed that they had to because they feared that some leukemic cells had already entered the spinal area, although it didn't show in the spinal taps. But they chose to be safe rather than sorry."

"Did you feel that it was experimental medicine or did you believe in what was going on?"

"I had a gut feeling that I didn't want him to have to go through that. I didn't like it. Every time I took him to the radiation area and watched him go into one of those machines, I felt sick to my stomach. It's easy for me to say that now, and it may have been the thing that saved Jason's life, I don't know, but the fact is by the next year, the doctors stopped doing cranial radiation. At the time, however, I didn't have the courage to trust my instincts. I trusted the professionals.

"There were so many times like this. Once they asked us if they could put Jason on a protocol that was being studied nationwide. Some kids got one treatment and some kids got another, and maybe some got placebos. They asked if we would agree to do it. They said we wouldn't know what protocol Jason was on until after the study was over, because it would all be computerized and random. But I decided I wasn't about to do that. Again, my gut instincts said, 'I want to know which drugs are the best for my son, and that's what I want him to have. I just won't take a chance.'

"It's mind-boggling how many drugs Jason has taken. He was taking Vincristine and Adriamycin—which is still being used. They gave up on Vincristine because it is highly toxic. He has had Cytoxan. He has taken a drug with a long name that they used to call MP-6. And for a long time they gave him steroids. The theory was that steroids build up the reproduction of the immature white cells and then the doctors blast all of them with chemo. That supposedly kills everything that's bad. I always wondered how many good things it killed, too. We know what steroids have done over the last few years to athletes. Think about guys like Lyle Alzado.

"We got through the difficult two weeks after Christmas, and then, amazingly, we fell into a routine. The doctors were able to stabilize Jason's white cell count, even though during the two and one half years he was on chemo, it was always horribly messed up. At that point, we could go home at night and come back during the day."

"How long did Jason stay in the hospital during this time?" I asked.

"Well, Grant turned one on January 24, and we wheeled Jason out into the garden at the hospital, in a little hospital cart and gave him a cupcake with one candle in it. It was awful to look at him. Jason had dropped to twenty-five pounds. He was just skin and bones. He couldn't walk. He had absolutely no meat on any part of his body, and his hair had fallen out. His eyes—oh, his eyes, they were like saucers. He looked like a little malnourished third-world child. But it was Grant's first birthday and we wanted them to share it. I think we brought Jason home the next week."

"Where was Grant during all of this?" I asked.

"He'd gone to stay with his grandparents. I've always felt horrible about that because this was a formative time for Grant, too. Mike and I had to focus so totally on Jason. I sometimes feel that Jason, by design or instinct, is such a phenomenal big brother because he is trying to repay the other boys for the time they lost. He really worries about them and he is the strong, mature young man in our family."

"Can you describe your day-to-day emotions?"

"I was robotic. I blocked my feelings. If I cried, I thought I'd never stop. So I just went about the daily process of coping with this horrendous disease as best I could, doing what the professionals told me, and just trying to hold on."

"Did Jason know how sick he was?"

"I'm not sure if anybody really knows that. He was only four years old. A lot of parents and some professionals think that kids have an instinct about that. If Jason's instincts told him how sick he was, he didn't let on to us; maybe that's part of being Texan. But he never complained. One story during this period really sums up how courageous these kids can be. One afternoon, Jason went to have another bone marrow. My mom and dad were visiting, so he asked if his grandfather could go with him. Jason told my dad that he wanted him to go because he couldn't stand to see me cry. It was very difficult for my father, but they went together. They had to sit facing each other cross-legged at maximum stillness while the bone marrow transplant was going on. My father held Jason's hands and helped keep his head still.

"Jason said to Dad through gritted teeth, 'Grandfather, I don't cry. I'm not going to cry.' And yet, when my father looked at him, there were huge tears rolling down his cheeks. But Jason still insisted, 'See, grandfather, I don't cry. I don't ever cry.' The courage of children—it makes us proud, and it makes us cry. My father never forgot that."

"Diana, what's the theory behind taking the marrow from the bone in the transplants?"

"Well, they pull marrow out of the hip joint because that's where the white cells are produced. So it's the best place to get an accurate sense of whether or not they're getting to the source of the leukemia. You gain your 'all clear' from chemo when you show up negative in the marrow."

"Okay, I need to backtrack a little. You've gone through this first crisis. You've taken Jason home and now, I suppose, you start the day-to-day living, right?"

"The word the doctors use when they talk about Jason's

chemotherapy is 'protocol,' and I think that's a good term to describe what my days were like. I began to develop a protocol, an operational approach to the problem from the time I spent with Grant, to the time I gave my business, to the time Mike and I spent together. Everything had to be planned. Yet against that, we never knew how Jason would be from day to day. His schedule dominated our lives. It defined what we did, how we thought, when we ate, and when we slept. There always was Jason's illness.

"We'd go to the hospital once a week for blood counts and my stomach would knot up. I used to feel like I needed to throw up. Every week I'd wait for the doctors to tell me how Jason was doing. They would take his blood count and say, 'Well, it doesn't look good this week.' So, they'd alter the chemo. And we would go once a month for bone marrows, and they'd say, 'Oh, we see something here. It doesn't look good.' Sometimes they would say, 'We've really made some progress here.' And I would feel as if I had jumped a hurdle, and then I would try to live the rest of my life as naturally as I could. I tried to make the natural things important, or maybe I ought to say that I tried to make the natural things normal.

"When Jason was home and stable, we needed to allow him to live a normal boy's life if we were going to have any hope for his future. We even let him go back to preschool when he could. That was tough because physically he didn't look at all like he did before. He'd gone from being a beautiful, healthy, round-faced, big-eyed, blond-haired boy to being a gaunt, bald-headed little character. The kids in preschool were tough on him. At that age, it's not that kids say a lot, it's that they laugh a lot. But Jason hung in there. He always wanted to go to preschool."

"You know, Diana, I think that's not just the will to survive. It indicates that we are truly an integrated species. We want to be with our own kind, no matter what the circumstance."

"I think you're right, Tom. Not only is there the will to live, but there is the will to participate, and Jason certainly had that."

"Can a parent tell when a child with leukemia is getting better?"

"No. That's one of the odd parts of the disease. There's no way to know any of that, and that's what made every week so difficult. When we would go for the blood workup or the monthly bone marrow check, we would have to rely on the professionals to tell us. Once Jason's condition stabilized, he began growing and gaining weight. Even though he had the hair loss related to his chemo, he seemed to be getting better. Yet I knew that could all end with the next blood test, in that moment when the doctor can't look into your eyes and has to tell you your child is worse again. I can remember sitting in that waiting room with cotton mouth and a lump in my stomach, just waiting to be called in. In fact, now that Jason is seventeen and we go for his yearly testing, I still feel exactly the same emotions and the same physical sensation in my stomach."

"Diana, do you think Mike was feeling the same things in this early period?"

"Mike took the position that was best for him: this is not going to happen to my son, I won't allow it. I'm going to draw a line in the sand and the disease won't get any further. So he seemed to live his life much more normally than I did."

"Was he in denial?" I asked.

"I think so, but I don't want to give the impression that he wasn't totally involved and a great father for Jason. He was always there. I just think he had a different way of coping with it than I did. Maybe that was because I was a part of the day-to-day process and he got involved more as a crisis-intervention parent. Again, to be fair, that's probably just the way it is with parents when they deal with disability or illness."

"I think so," I said. "I'm finding that parents take on individually appropriate roles based on circumstances. The parents

I've been talking to go through a frantic period in which they learn as much as possible about the disability. They all seem to panic when they think about whether their children are being treated or educated in the right way. Did you have those kinds of panic emotions over Jason?"

"Oh, it was unbelievable. Here this little boy was having all of these chemo protocols—chemo seemed like a mystery to me anyway—and I kept wondering if he was with good doctors and in the right facility. Then, one day, one of the nurses said to me, 'You ought to have Jason at St. Jude's. That's the only place to be.' I heard that, and I panicked. I started reading every magazine article and book that had anything to do with the treatment for leukemia I could get my hands on. Then I started calling facilities like St. Jude's and Scripps Institute and the Mayo Clinic, to get some answers. Thank God I had a cousin who was a physician. He helped me follow up on every lead. And he finally said that Jason was getting the best possible treatment at Children's. With the new cooperation of physician groups in oncology, he had no doubt that Jason was benefiting from the most up-to-date information and chemo available, but you feel like chemo is a crap shoot. I mean, remember that list of drugs I told you about, and there were many more. You think to yourself, 'Here is a four-year-old boy on probably eight different drugs along with the steroids.' And you panic because you have to sit in that waiting room and know that there isn't a thing you can do about helping the condition of your child. It just breaks your heart, your spirit—it actually breaks you down physically. I felt lousy. There were times when I wondered about my own health."

"What about help during this time, Diana? Did you have a network of helping friends?"

"I've always been lucky about friends. Maybe I'm one of those people who draws them, but I've always had a fantastic group of friends to share with."

"But what about parent networking? Were you a participant in parent organizations?"

"I think parents fall into two categories. There are those who really need the networking. They talk about the issues constantly with each other. And then, there are the ones who, I suppose, are loners. They just don't see a lot of value in those interactions. I belong to the second type. Jason was like that, too. He never wanted to participate in activities that involved other kids with cancer. I think maybe both of us were aware that a lot of the children in these groups were dying. In fact, many did die. So for us that was too personal. I also decided that having as normal a life as possible was the very best thing we could do for Jason. We treated going to the doctor as something we just had to do that day. When we finished the examination and walked out the door, we went on about living our lives. But I don't want you to think that I didn't need anybody. There were some remarkably special people who helped us. One is the head of oncology at the hospital, George Buchanan. He has become well known nationally as a researcher on the forefront of children's cancers."

"What made him special for you?" I asked.

"He had the ability to create instant rapport. He seemed to know just what to say to each parent and how much they could handle. In my case, he got me busy.

"One day I told him that when we got past the current crisis I wanted to give something back for all the help we'd been given. So as Jason progressed, Dr. Buchanan asked me if I'd help him form a fund-raising organization at Children's Hospital geared specifically to children's cancer research needs. He wanted to bring in research fellows who would do special work for children. He also hoped that the hospital would develop an expanded treatment center. And I said I'd be delighted to do that for him. So we started what's now the Children's Cancer Fund of Dallas. We began from the tiniest recruitment drive and it has grown tremendously. This year, we raised between four and five million dollars. The Cancer Fund has grown far beyond any dreams I might have had, and that's a wonderful feeling for me. Though I wasn't a parent joiner, I do feel good that I gave something back.

"Dr. Buchanan and I were only two of the three people who started the fund. The other person was a dad—a very special father—who had lost his child, and that really brought the reality of life and death home. I figured out that if you've competed with death long enough—that is, competed to keep someone you love alive—everything else in life seems incidental. The fact that Mike and I got divorced and I'm raising four boys is difficult, but it all seems like a piece of cake compared to life and death."

"That's how I feel about blindness," I said. "Once I learned how to handle that, everything else seemed easy. I think they call that perspective." We both thought about that for a minute.

Diana said, "Perspective is a good word. I suppose I really came to understand the twists and turns of life after Jason had finished his first protocol. They gave him a clean bill of health—no sign of leukemia in the marrow. We really thought we had beaten it, and then the world fell apart again."

"What happened?" I asked.

"We had finished the protocol, and Jason had been home a month. Things were going well. He was in the second grade—imagine that, Tom, he'd made it to the second grade—when he started to feel ill. He developed what we thought was croup. Then he developed a high fever that got higher and higher. In the middle of the night, Mike went in to check on him, and found that Jason's eyes had completely rolled back in his head. He had had a seizure. It scared us to death. We grabbed him and rushed to the hospital. He was totally flaccid. He even lost his bowels as we picked him up. I couldn't believe this was happening. I had to call friends at three in the morning to find someone to watch Grant. Thank God I had such good friends. By the time we got to the hospital, he had awakened, but they checked him in anyway. But, so many things happened during this stay. First of all, Children's in Dallas is a teaching hospital, and that means that there are interns and residents who constantly migrate through the hospital's wards, really bothering you because they have to learn as much as they can. I tried to understand. I'd been real patient with these people, but at that moment, we weren't ready to handle any kind of personal invasion.

"I remember an intern came in and asked all kinds of questions about Jason's history. I took an immediate dislike to this doctor. And this was a turning point for me, because for the first time, I trusted my own parental instincts. I felt this man was young and arrogant. Somebody decided that Jason needed an immediate bone marrow and spinal tap, so they wheeled him down to where these tests were going to be run. The intern came in with an incredible attitude. He looked at Jason and the first thing he said was, 'Well, I'm going to do this bone marrow and spinal tap today. Gee, I haven't done one of these in a long time.' My heart stopped. Normally, in a hospital situation, most people feel that they can't say 'No, you're not! I don't care who you are, you're not going to touch my child.' But, I did.

"He said, 'What do you mean?'

"And I told him, 'I want Jason taken back to his room. I've got some phone calls to make.'

"'Oh, I was just kidding,' he said.

"'I don't care what you're telling me now, Doctor, he's not going to have this procedure done by you. So take us back to our room.'

"Very reluctantly, and with a cold shoulder from the nurses who had prepared for the procedure—along with everybody else that had been put out by my tantrum—they took Jason back to the room. I called George Buchanan, head of oncology at Children's, and I told him exactly what had transpired. This young doctor never appeared on the floor again. George came in and apologized profusely. He made it clear that we would absolutely never see this young doctor involved with Jason.

"I learned that you can influence the outcome. If you've got a gut instinct, and you're the parent of a sick child, follow that instinct, and just say no. It doesn't matter who is inconvenienced. To this day, I'm convinced that I was right. Parents have to be the bottom line, the final decision-makers."

"I'm glad you said that, Diana. I'm hearing that a lot as I'm working on this book. So you believe, from that time on, you became a different kind of parent?"

"I sure do, Tom! When Jason was in the hospital with the seizures and croup, this was the single most frightening experience we had had to go through. Even though the doctors weren't telling us that Jason's leukemia had returned, croup could have killed him just as easily. When a child has croup, he wheezes and his vocal cords swell. He can't breathe, and there is an ongoing cough. The doctors usually put the child in a tent-like device with humidifiers on the inside to help ease breathing. Generally, the swelling comes down after a while, and most kids do all right. But, remember, for Jason any infection could kill him, because he had no immunity.

"The hospital was faced with a difficult dilemma. They should have put Jason in the intensive care unit so they could watch him, listen to him breathe, and make sure that he was remaining stable. However, there was a child dying from a critical case of Reye syndrome in the intensive care unit at that time. Reye syndrome is due to chicken pox, which can quickly kill children who are immunosuppressed. In fact, children who are immunosuppressed have been experimentally given a chicken pox vaccine, a gamma globulin chemical compound that was only available in Japan. Later, Jason got this vaccine so that he wouldn't be vulnerable to chicken pox while he was on chemotherapy.

"But, in the meantime, the doctors were not sure what to do. They could put Jason in ICU, knowing full well that the staff was moving from child to child, and there was a chance that someone would carry something somehow to Jason from this other child. They decided that was not a risk they wanted to take. But, they couldn't take the other little boy out of the intensive care unit either. So they chose to put Jason in a tent in a regular hospital room.

"Mike and I became very concerned about this. We knew what happened at night—how very few nurses were left on the floor—and nobody would be able to monitor Jason on a consistent basis. We didn't think we could stay awake all night either. We'd been up for several days and nights in a row with a very sick child, and we were exhausted. Our judgment wasn't very good, so Mike hired a very expensive private nurse to be there during the night. After she arrived, we felt pretty relaxed. She never left Jason's side. She was monitoring him, and he seemed to be okay. At about midnight, we'd fallen asleep in chairs next to Jason's bed, and the respiratory therapist came in and said, 'Well, I think Jason is doing much better.' But we could hear his breathing and we just didn't buy that. We told him so, and he thought we were crazy. We looked at each other, and we wondered if we were crazy because the respiratory therapist told us that Jason was better. The nurse was right there, and she didn't seem alarmed. Again, as parents, we doubted ourselves. So, we sat back down in our chairs and dozed off.

"No, wait a minute, Tom, wait a minute, what actually happened was that we even called the resident who was on duty, and she came in and she listened to Jason's breathing and she said, 'Oh, he's doing a lot better!' So we did lean back in our chairs, and we dozed.

"At seven A.M., the shift changed. The new doctors and nursing staff came on and the night shift went home. The new day nurse came onto the floor, and our private duty nurse was still standing there, checking what we thought were Jason's vital signs. I was just waking up and watching as this young, spry girl came bouncing in. She went up to Jason, and took his pulse, and then put her stethoscope on his chest. I saw absolute disbelief come into her eyes. Without saying a word, she ran from the room, and started shouting in the hallway. The next minute, we heard 'Code Blue Emergency!' We could hear the pounding of people's feet as they came running down the hall. They ran into the room and grabbed Jason right out of bed. I saw his head just flop over the arms of one of the residents, and his legs were limp. He was like a rag doll. They ran out of the room, and told us to stay where we were.

"I kept saying, 'My God, what's going on, what's going on?'

"And someone said, 'We're not getting a pulse—we're not finding a heartbeat.' And I can remember that moment in time as if it were happening right now. I can remember everything that was said.

"I went back, sat in the room and just rocked in my chair, frantically praying as hard and as loud as I could, 'Please, God, don't let this happen to my little boy, please.' And we were just two people stuck there with our son down the hall, not knowing if he was dead or alive. There was nothing we could do. We couldn't be with him.

"Thank God, we had some luck. George Levies, our pediatrician, showed up at precisely that moment to make his early morning rounds. At the same time, an anesthesiologist, famous in children's oncology, was also coming up to the floor to begin a procedure. As he was coming up the elevator, he heard the code call. He came running down the hall to see if he could do anything to help, so at least there were two great doctors there. After a while, our pediatrician walked into our room with tears in his eyes. He was shaking his head. He looked at us and said, 'We just don't know; they're doing the best they can. We just don't know. They say he's fighting it, he's fighting it.'

"I have no idea how long we were there. It must have been a while, because some of our friends showed up. I don't know who called them or how they got there, but they were there.

"Finally, staff members came in and told us that they were moving Jason to the ICU. They had to move him there, even though the other boy had chicken pox. I saw him being moved. They had slashed his wrists and they were pumping in adrenaline to try to get his heart going again. And this absolutely wonderful anesthesiologist was forcing a trach down Jason's windpipe. His throat had completely closed up with the croup and this doctor saved his life. That's why Jason has such a scratchy voice now. They began to get some breathing response.

"They finally came back in to us and said, 'He has been unconscious. He could be brain dead. We have no way of knowing, because we don't know how long he was out.'

"The agonizing just went on hour after hour. We sat there waiting to be told what the outcome was. And then they finally came down again, and said, 'We're going to take you up to the ICU. Jason is awake, and he's alert, but we want to prepare you for the fact that he may not know who you are.' They didn't know if the damage was so extensive, his memory might have been lost, or what else might be wrong. They only knew that he was alive.

"We walked into the unit not knowing whether our beloved child would even recognize us. I remember looking over at this little frail figure strapped down—they do this to children so they don't pull the tubes out of their mouths—and he said 'M-o-h-h-m-m-m,' in a little scratchy voice. I knew he recognized me, and I thought, 'He'll be all right, and from now on we can deal with anything, because we've been to hell and back. We've seen the worst that life can deal out, and we're still here and Jason's still here. We'll cope with whatever happens together.'

"But from that time on, my faith in medicine was shaken. They missed the diagnosis—all of them missed the diagnosis—and they are responsible for that. I now view doctors on an individual basis. There are good ones and bad ones. I trust my instincts to find the good ones.

"Subsequently, Jason developed pneumonia. Do you believe that? And they were really concerned then, because it was the same pneumonia AIDS patients get. I didn't know there were different kinds of pneumonia. So he was in the ICU with that, and everybody had to dress in sterile gowns and wear masks. It all became like a horrible costume party, where nobody was real. I suppose Death was probably the special guest. And on this ward, I had heard that there were children who died as a result of contracting AIDS through transfusions of contaminated blood. So over the years, I thanked God that we were a lucky family, and that Jason was spared."

"Diana, did you ever express the kind of anger you must have felt toward the hospital?"

"I never really did. I know parents often do, but I don't think that we can afford to burn all our bridges. We parents have to do what's right for our children. But we still have to work inside the system with some organized approach to other people's professionalism. We can't keep crying wolf, because after a while, people won't listen to us. It's important to pick the effective battleground. The hospital really sends parents a double message. On the one hand, even today, most hospitals don't provide support space for us to stay with our children when they are very sick, but on the other, the hospital wants us there to help with our child, because they don't have the personnel to deal with them all the time. This is one of my big gripes. I don't think that it has changed much in a lot of facilities now. The doctor may be the practitioner, but the parent is the provider of love, support, and care."

"Thanks for making that point, Diana. I know a lot of the readers are going to be glad to hear it."

"I hope so. While I'm on my soapbox, let me tell you about the problem with teaching hospitals. I know these young doctors have to learn, but it has to be governed better. Parents just can't keep answering the same questions over and over again so that one of these young doctors can fill out his or her chart. Hospitals have to care for parents along with treating the child, and parents can't take that kind of emotional strain. We're just trying to hold on; that's all we can do."

"Diana, as Jason is growing, does he talk about the disease?"

"He never really has. I think part of that was because we were so conscious of making sure that he continued to live as normal a life as we could provide. Now that he's seventeen, and we go back for his once-a-year checkup, he's a hero to a lot of the kids who are at Children's. Very often I hear them say to him, 'Are you still sick?' And he says, 'No, I'm fine now. I did have leukemia like you, but I'm fine now.' I can see him warm to these children, and I love to see the hope in their eyes. It's a touching moment. We never did talk about Jason's illness very much with him. Actually, he talks about it more today than he ever did before. It's almost becoming part of his biographical description. I do wonder sometimes what he thinks about when he considers his future; and now that I've talked to you, I'm going to ask him if he still thinks he could get sick. Actually, though we've learned a lot about the success rate with kids like Jason, there really isn't anything that's absolute when you deal with leukemia."

"But obviously, Diana, Jason is still here, so you got

through the first two and a half years of chemo. Can you remember the moment when you went to the doctors and they said Jason was clear?"

"Oh, yes. It's another one of those moments you never lose. The funny part of it is that we had been so involved, day after day after day, with this sickness, that when we were given the 'all clear' we didn't go crazy, we didn't jump up and down and celebrate. We just sighed and tried to find a way back to living our lives as normally as possible."

"So what was normal for you?" I asked.

"Well, I got pregnant again. And I'd have to say that overall this was a wonderful period for our family. We didn't even think of death as often. It started to slip away, and Jason went back to school. His hair grew back, and with the exception of his voice, his life became pretty normal. He got through that year and we were beginning to get excited. I started to use phrases like 'Maybe it's all over,' or 'I don't think it will ever happen again,' or 'We beat the odds, didn't we?' We even moved from Dallas, down to Mexia, Texas. Mexia is a small rural town. It's a safe place to raise kids, and we wanted that for our boys. We wanted a stress-free life. We would never have moved if we had thought Jason would get sick again, because Mexia is a couple of hours from Dallas. But we really were sure. Mike was beginning to succeed in his law practice, so even though I had to give up my business, our lives were wonderful.

"A year and a half went by and we had no problems. A lot of kids relapse right after they come out of chemo, and when they do, most of them die. Some relapse, maybe six months after chemo, and even more of them die. But Jason relapsed a year and a half out of chemo. Children who relapsed, at that time, usually died."

"Diana, you'd gone through this year and a half, and everything was O.K. What happened? How did you learn about this horrible turnaround?"

"We went up to Dallas for Jason's normal check, and oddly enough Mike chose to come with us. He usually didn't come, but Jason was going to have a bone marrow that day and he wanted to have his dad there. When Jason came out after the scan Dr. Buchanan asked for Mike and me to come to his office. As we were walking, I thought, 'This has to be bad news.' Sure enough, Dr. Buchanan said, 'We detect traces of leukemia in the bone marrow again, and Jason has officially relapsed.'

"'What does that mean?' I asked.

"And he said, 'We have to start all over again. It's like the first part never happened, because the chemo didn't work. We're going to have to give him the most intensively invasive treatments we possibly can, and we're going to use the most successful combinations that have ever been tried for children with relapse, but I can't promise you anything. His chances of survival have dropped from seventy percent to thirty percent, and I have to say that's being optimistic. The fact is, his chances are very slim.'

"In all honesty this day was more devastating than the first, because we had believed Jason was fully recovered, and we now knew what we were in for. We also knew the chances of survival were small, and we simply had no more strength. In that respect, I think Jason's will to live was much stronger than my belief that he would. I was shattered. I remember we went to have lunch somewhere, and nobody talked. But now we had to talk to Jason because he was eight, and could understand all this. He knew what he was in for. He was involved emotionally because he knew how severe it all was. And so we were all broken-hearted.

"What's worse, we now lived one hundred miles from the treatment center, and that meant an incredibly complex commute. We would drive up to Dallas early in the morning and Jason would get his medicine. And then, because of the pain, the nurses would have to give him something to put him to sleep for the ride home so he wouldn't suffer in any way. That became our weekly journey for the next two years.

"Our greatest crisis during that two-year period—until Jason made it to the fifth grade—did not even relate to the leukemia. It related to the steroid prednisone that Jason was taking. He had developed a craving for chips, popcorn, and salted peanuts. Even though I had gained all of this knowledge about leukemia, nobody told me that steroids caused the desire for salt in children. Because of this, he had eaten too much salt, and his blood pressure went up. He was due to go back to Dallas one day for his checkup, and amazingly, it was another time that Mike went with us. Mike and Jason stopped on the way up to get something to eat. I'm not sure what he had eaten, but by the time they pulled into Children's Hospital, Jason had fallen asleep. Mike shook him but couldn't awaken him.

"I didn't hear about it right away, because I drove separately. I pulled in and parked. As I walked in, the first thing I heard was the paging system: 'STAT—for Dr. Buchanan. Please come to Emergency.' I knew that Dr. Buchanan was Jason's doctor, and I couldn't find Jason and Mike. Then I heard the nurses talking about a little boy, and I just ran into Emergency. Once again Jason was unconscious; he'd had another seizure, related to the blood pressure this time. They worked and worked and worked on him, and I thought we were losing him again. They kept telling us they didn't know how long he had been unconscious. They started to talk about brain damage, and I nearly went out of my mind. Thank God, it didn't last as long. They brought him around more quickly. But I just felt like my life was hanging by a thread.

"At the time, I was very pregnant with Adam, our fourth child, and I kept saying to myself, 'I've got to stay calm because I've got a baby coming real soon, and I've got a responsibility to that baby. I have a responsibility to the boys at home.' I had to make myself settle down. Somehow we got through it, but you never come out of a crisis without injury. In this case, Jason developed hepatitis."

"Oh, my God," I said, "how could that have happened?"

"Nobody knows. Jason has hepatitis C. It's noncontagious, and none of the doctors know when he acquired it. But recently, when he was in for a checkup, some insensitive intern told him that the new hospital protocol required that patients with hepatitis be tested for AIDS. I lost it. 'Jason isn't even sexually active, and you want him to take an AIDS test?' I said. 'Why is that? Because you messed up, because years ago he might have had tainted blood, because you are trying to cover your ass? Jason doesn't have to take an AIDS test. There is no law, there's no requirement. I'm not going to let you give him an AIDS test.'"

"Diana, now that Jason is seventeen, do you think he should have had the test?"

"Tom, if down the line Jason wants to be tested for AIDS, it's his business, but I know he is perfectly fine. They ran HIV tests on his blood before it was considered a requirement, so I know he's fine. I just didn't like the idea that by implication, a hospital could be that demanding. It's another one of those moments when you become a Parent Advocate."

"Diana, we haven't talked much about the social aspect of his disease. Jason got through this relapse over the next two years. So he'd be in the fifth grade, right?"

"That's right, and this was a tough social time for him when he went back to school. He lost his hair right at the end of the chemo. He hadn't grown as fast as the other kids, and he had that difficulty with his voice. So when he would be with the kids in class, he didn't want them to see his head. He always kept a baseball hat on. The school let him except when he went out for the basketball team. He's a good little player. I'll always remember his first game, when the coach told him he had to take his hat off to play. He didn't do it until just when the whistle blew. But you know, he hung in there and he played.

There were times when the kids would laugh at him, but his friends came to his defense. I even think they beat up some of the kids who laughed at him. At the end of that year, Jason received the 'Most Outstanding Student' award for his school. What a wonderful moment for that little boy, and for us. And now, you know him, Tom; you know he's flourishing."

"I do know he's flourishing, Diana. I know he is tall and handsome and happy. And you're doing better, too, right?"

"I am. I've got the same kind of business going again, and it's beginning to grow. I don't think I live with Death as my copilot anymore. In fact, I know I don't, because instead of seeing Jason as a sick little boy, I now see him as a very difficult teenager, with raging hormones and his own opinions, and a bright future."

CHAPTER

Karen and Arthur

OFTEN SIGHTED FRIENDS have asked me how I could possibly deal with the disability of blindness. I find myself laughing because that's simply the only state of the human condition I've ever known. For me, blindness is a way of life. But over the years, I've found that I often responded to the question by telling people that I don't think I would be capable of coping with deafness. The idea of not listening to the sounds of summer birds or a Mozart symphony or, especially, the laughter of a child seems impossible for me to accept. Yet I have had many deaf friends who feel just the opposite. The concept that their eyes couldn't do the job frightens them. Probably the only objective source, in fact, maybe the only umpire who could answer this question, was Helen Keller.

I had the chance to meet Ms. Keller on the occasion of her eightieth birthday, at the Perkins School for the Blind, when I was about eight years old. She had come back to her place of education to receive a birthday tribute. I still remember that when she addressed all of the students, she told us that her hearing was the sense she missed the most.

I'm bringing all this up because you're about to meet a marvelous family who are successfully raising a terrific child who is deaf, and who have found an educational system that works. So far, you may have felt that this book was slanted toward criticizing the systems of education that come to bear on the lives of all people with disabilities. It seemed to me significant, then, to take a look at a family coping with what I consider to be the most difficult of disabilities, in a very exciting and positive way.

Karen and Arthur Jokela live in the beautiful ranch community of Thousand Oaks, California, with two boys uniquely named Mars and Cosmo, names carefully chosen to define them as special. It is a second marriage for both, and they believe family has taken on even more importance the second time around.

"Karen, when you had Mars, was there anything unusual about the pregnancy?"

"Not really, Tom, except that I was pretty old." We all laughed.

"Mars's pregnancy was perfect. He came into the world pretty easily, and actually that's the last easy thing he's ever done. He's a gifted child."

"Really," I said.

"Tom, I think it's actually much more difficult for a gifted child to find his place. Certainly the educational opportunities are more limited, and the socialization process is very complicated."

"I'll bet," I said. "So Mars was four years old when Cosmo was born, right?"

"That's right," Karen said. "But I was four years older, and this pregnancy was much more difficult."

"Did anything unusual happen?" I asked.

Karen wasn't laughing now. "The birth was complicated. His head didn't want to turn, so that it could be easily pulled out. Cosmo just didn't seem to want to be born. My water hadn't broken yet, so he had the first stool, called *meconium* in utero, and he breathed it into his lungs, causing real problems."

"What happened?" I asked.

"Well, the doctors had to resuscitate him," Karen said. "I know that many parents go through those moments when their babies don't breathe, but I'll never forget it. You hang by a thread, waiting to see what fate will decide."

"I remember that," Arthur told me. "You see, being a scientist, I need to always feel that there are answers, that I can complete things, that there is closure. Yet in this case, all we could do was watch and hope that the doctors knew what they were doing."

"Arthur, are you comfortable with the way Cosmo was treated by the physicians?"

"Totally, Tom," Arthur said. "He had to stay in intensive care over the next couple of weeks. The doctors and the whole staff were wonderful to us. At a time when people are screaming about malpractice, it's great to be able to say that Cosmo's care was wonderful."

"Arthur, that's not quite how I remember it," Karen said. "I know that the care was wonderful, but I can never forget the fact that the doctors told us there was only a fifty-fifty chance that Cosmo would live. I don't want Tom to get the impression that this was just a picnic."

"I didn't get that impression," I said. "Karen, at the end of the two weeks in intensive care, what did the doctors tell you when it was time for you to take Cosmo home?"

"They gave us some 'preventative antibiotics,' which are what eventually caused Cosmo's deafness."

"Wait a minute!" I said. "You just told me that the doctors

did a great job. Now you're telling me that the antibiotics caused Cosmo's deafness."

"That's right." Arthur was speaking now, and I could tell that this admission pained him. "Science just isn't perfect," he said. "Maybe the antibiotics caused Cosmo to be deaf, yet without them, he might not have lived. There wasn't much of a choice."

I thought about that. "I understand what you're talking about," I said. "I was born in 1947, three months premature, and I was placed in an incubator to provide me with the oxygen I needed to live. Unfortunately, I got too much oxygen, and that caused the condition that made me blind. Yet if I had been born a year earlier, I wouldn't have survived, even the first day of life. So I suppose there are trade-offs. But they have to be extremely difficult trade-offs."

"Not really," Karen said. "When I look at this wonderfully alive boy now, I don't see the trade-off as complicated at all. All I see is that we have a terrific son. I also should tell you that the doctors did inform us, in advance, that the antibiotic might cause a little deafness. That's a funny phrase, 'a little deafness.' I don't know that you can be a little anything. I mean, you're not a little blind, are you?"

I laughed. "Nope, blind as a bat," I said. "That's the only way I've ever lived."

"So I guess this means, Tom, that the doctors still have to grow both in knowledge and sensitivity. Because of the way the doctor said it, I didn't really come to understand that Cosmo was deaf for a long time, or maybe I denied it."

"Let's explore this concept a little more," I said. "Arthur, you're a scientist. Where's the relationship between good science, or maybe I could say, realism, and hope?"

"Well, they're both clearly part of what goes on in the mind of a parent, when you're in this kind of stressful period. Everything is happening all around you. The doctors are busy, people are running in and out. The first days are a blur. And even though a doctor may tell you that your child may be facing 'a little deafness,' some combination of hope and numbness keeps you from really hearing him. The fact that Karen didn't even consider deafness as part of Cosmo's existence until he was eighteen months old means that we never really heard what the doctor said—and the fact that we remember it proves that premise wrong—or we chose to ignore what he said. I frankly think that's far more likely."

"Karen, why did the medication cause deafness?" I asked.

"One of the side effects of gentamicin is that the hairs in the inner ear, and the cochlea, become damaged. That condition leads to deafness."

"After the two weeks of intensive care, you brought Cosmo home. Can either of you remember your first sense that you might have a deaf child?"

"We were completely different when it came to this issue," Arthur said. "I knew quite early, but I never really talked to Karen about it. I can remember that I would walk up behind Cosmo's head and clap my hands loudly and he never responded. I'm sure I did that because I had already sensed that he wasn't being particularly verbal or trying to create interesting sounds. I knew by the time he was eight or nine months that he was quite likely deaf."

"I didn't feel the same way at all," Karen said. "In fact, when Cosmo was supposed to go back to the pediatrician for an appointment at nine months, I cancelled it, because I told the doctor that everything was just perfect. He was crawling and climbing up and down the stairs with no problem. His motor skills were wonderful. I knew that he wasn't making any sounds that could be interpreted as a search for language, but I was sure he was a perfectly normal child in every way. I guess I have to admit I was in complete denial." Karen turned to Arthur. "Arthur, why didn't you say anything to me about this?"

"I did, dear, you just weren't listening."

"I don't remember that at all," she said.

"Karen, you know I had to have the data supported; I had to know if my impression, my hunch, that Cosmo was deaf, could be validated."

"And we talked about it?" she said.

"A lot," Arthur told her.

"So when did you actually know, Karen? When did *you* find out that Cosmo was, in fact, deaf?" I asked.

"When he went back to the pediatrician for his checkup at a year and a half."

"By eighteen months most children are talking. Cosmo wasn't, right?"

"That's right," Karen said.

"And he wasn't indicating any interest in defining his verbal skills, right?"

"I know it sounds absurd, Tom, but as I said, I was in complete denial."

"So what happened in the doctor's office?" I asked.

"He recommended an audiology exam. We went to the exam, and right there, the audiologist told us that Cosmo had a profound hearing loss."

"That he was deaf?" I asked.

"I don't know if she used that word," Karen said.

"She did," Arthur told me. "She said, 'Your son is profoundly deaf.'"

Karen laughed. "Maybe I'm still in some kind of denial. I know at the time I just didn't want to hear that word."

Arthur said, "I think we're being a little too dramatic. The fact was that we needed to come to terms with this analytical truth, and once we were clearly sure that the data was definite, that Cosmo was deaf, we got on with the process of living, of taking care of our child."

"You may have gotten on with the process, Arthur, but I was still in denial, and I had a lot to work through. It took me a long time."

"Karen, Arthur, as I've been writing this book, I've seen parents fill different places in their child's living equation. I've decided that that's the way it's supposed to be. Everyone, in one way or another, fills the spaces, the holes, for someone else. In your case, Arthur fulfills logic and science, and you, Karen, fulfilled the emotional requirements for your son."

"You mean I'm a wet noodle?" Karen laughed.

"No, no," I said. "Just think of it as filling in the spaces."

Arthur said, "You know, to carry this further within this scientific framework, we intentionally had these boys later in our lives. We knew there was a certain sense of risk, but we were willing to take it, because we weren't sure that our older sons from our previous marriages were ever going to give us grandchildren, and frankly, we wanted to have that part of our lives fulfilled."

"Is that a selfish concept?" I asked.

"I don't think so," Karen said. "I admit that sometimes in that early period, I felt horrible guilt, particularly after I'd found out that Cosmo was deaf. But remember, this was only eight years ago, and science had come a long way. Many women in their early forties were having children. I wasn't so unusual. And I've always been strong and extremely healthy."

"The statistics were very much on our side," Arthur said. "You have to live with a balance between statistical analysis and, well, let me call it the human factor. We wanted these boys, and we're incredibly grateful we have them."

"Karen, I'm curious. When I was interviewing a family with a blind child, the mother told me that she often fooled herself about the idea that her child was blind. She said that she used to wave a light in front of his eyes, and tell her husband that he was following it. When you were in denial, did you do things like that? Did you try to fool yourself about Cosmo's deafness?"

"I sure did. Cosmo was diagnosed at the end of June, and in July, we moved from California to Minnesota. The doctors told me, 'When you get there, call the local school district, and they'll get you in touch with the preschool teacher who is assigned to handling deaf kids for your area.' My oldest son was with me at the time. He was sixteen, and I was involved in a custody battle with his father. I didn't do a damn thing about Cosmo until December. During all that time, I kept saying, 'Oh, he hears.' And I was finding little incidents that said, 'See, he had to hear that.'

"Thank goodness a wonderful early-intervention teacher in Minnesota was assigned to Cosmo after he had had his first audiological profile. Her name was Cathy, and she didn't take any garbage from me at all. While I was trying to tell her that Cosmo could hear, she was saying, 'Well, we'll see, but for right now, let's get him the appropriate equipment, and let's start to teach you sign language.'"

"So you began to learn sign language before you had accepted the idea that Cosmo was deaf."

"I did, and I'm grateful to Cathy for taking such a proactive stand."

"Arthur, did you begin to learn sign language at this point, also?"

"Yes, I did, Tom, because I had already accepted the idea that Cosmo was deaf."

Karen said, "It's amazing. You probably heard this from other parents, but you do grab at straws. I was reading articles on every disability that might relate to Cosmo. For example, I read everything I could get my hands on about autism. It seemed to me that that might be another logical possibility. Then I talked to nutritionists about altering Cosmo's diet, thinking that might help him. Frankly, I don't think I got all these demons under control until Cosmo was almost two. But I remember the moment I came to understand his deafness as clearly as if it were yesterday."

"Really?" I said. "When was that?"

"We were all outside by the swimming pool on a hot summer day. Somebody was playing with a balloon right behind Cosmo, and it popped. You know how people usually react to a popping balloon: they jump. Cosmo didn't move. He didn't even acknowledge that anything had happened. That was the day that my balloon burst, too—I realized that Cosmo was truly deaf."

Arthur took her hand. "There always has to be hope." He was speaking to her. "That's what keeps the world spinning."

"Arthur," she laughed, "you really are a romantic. You're not just a scientist."

"Karen, when you finally had to deal with the reality of the deafness, did you grieve?"

"I did," she said. "I went through the whole process; in fact, when we moved back to California I must tell you that I was grieving all the way through the first year that we had Cosmo in the Tripod Program. I used to make a long commute down the mountains to the school. We weren't living in Los Angeles then. I even had an accident one morning, because I was involved in so much grieving."

Arthur said, "I know that some parents grieve, but I think it's superfluous. It doesn't achieve anything. It just wastes time and energy."

"That's pretty tough," I said.

"Cosmo is real, and his deafness is real. I believe that learning to cope with reality is our ultimate goal."

"Well, would you acknowledge that Karen had every reason to grieve?" I asked.

"Of course," Arthur said. "It just wasn't for me."

"Karen, you said your grief went on for quite a while. Can you describe in which ways it occurred?"

"The car accident was a prime example. I had the accident because I wasn't concentrating on the road. I was angry that Cosmo was deaf, and even more upset because I had to drive him to a special school."

"Again," I said, "I think you both found a balance that's appropriate to this family. I'm sure that's why Cosmo is doing so well today."

Arthur said, "There's another reason. I think I have something to do with it. I wasn't really paying the kind of attention I should have during my older sons' growing-up years. I was so involved in my own work, my scientific study. I don't think I gave them the kind of quality time I should have. I've spent a great deal of my life teaching, and I've found that teachers tend to be far better at instructing other kids than they are at teaching their own. As a consequence, when we found out that Cosmo was deaf, I saw this as a wonderful surprise and an opportunity to do a better job, to be involved. I think Cosmo has benefited from that commitment."

Karen said, "We've demonstrated many different parenting patterns than we did with the other boys. In the first place, Arthur's work always dominated where we lived and how we functioned. But in this case, we came back to California and found Tripod, the school that Cosmo now attends, because we learned that that's where Cosmo could get the best education. Within that system, he was able to involve himself in the Montessori teaching method, and he has benefited tremendously from the entire Tripod environment. So I think it's fair to say that we changed from parents who love their children by observation, that is to say, we observed and then carried out appropriate love or discipline, to parents who became very hands-on participants. And you know, Tom, that's a healthy change, and it wouldn't have happened had Cosmo not been deaf."

"Arthur, when we talked on the phone about this interview, I was struck that you credited Tripod, the school for the deaf here in Los Angeles, for much of Cosmo's success."

"Frankly, I don't have the words to tell you how important Tripod has been in our lives. You see, when we first came back to California, before we lived in Los Angeles, we lived up in the mountain town of Idyllwild. And the only available help for Cosmo then was either through very inadequate public school education, or through the State School for the Deaf. And to tell you the truth, it was horrible."

Karen said, "We wanted our son to have early intervention, but we didn't want him to have early isolation, and that's what happens in state schools."

"I know," I said. "Isolation is one of the major problems that confronts children with disabilities, and I think particularly the deaf."

"So," Arthur said, "we moved from Idyllwild to Los Angeles to be close to Tripod."

"Who referred you to Tripod?" I asked.

"The parent of another deaf child," Arthur said. "One of the most remarkable people we have ever met. She is truly a proactive parent, and she has not only stimulated us but started very powerful parent groups for the deaf that have really made a difference. Her name is Ginger Greeves, and she told us that Tripod was the only school she knew about that was searching for new and innovative methods to cope with the fundamental questions of deafness and communication."

"Cosmo was then about two years old, right?"

"That's right," Karen said.

"How were you communicating with him?"

"Well, I think right from the beginning, he understood

signs, and I don't mean just sign language. That really came later. He understood that he couldn't hear, and so he had to use signs to communicate. He has always been one of those children who seem to be able to adapt. Also," she said, "he was a discipline problem. He'd been independent right from the beginning, but I think the frustration with his deafness made him overreact to everything."

Arthur said, "I have been so impressed with Cosmo's ability to adapt. He has always been able to compensate, to find his own path to problem-solving. And though I agree with Karen—he has been very frustrated at times—for the most part, he has really understood that he must search harder than other people to get to the answers."

"I really don't understand it," I said, "but I know that there are people with disabilities who can compensate better than other human beings. I suppose it's what separates them. It's what makes some people winners and others people who live their lives struggling to find their place."

"That's right," Arthur said, "and Cosmo, well, he was always a winner."

"Did you have any trouble getting Cosmo into Tripod?" I asked.

Karen said, "Tom, do you know what IEP is?"

"I do," I said. "I've come across that with other parents during my interviews in the past. It stands for *Individual Education Plan*, right?"

"That's right," she said. "When Cosmo was first evaluated for preschool programs, we were not living in Los Angeles County, and the options for his early education were poor. Deafness is a lot like blindness. Children are categorized in two ways: they're either just deaf, or they are multi-disabled. The latter can include mental handicaps."

"So what did you do?"

"Well, we moved into Los Angeles County so that I could get Cosmo to Tripod. But still the drive was about an hour each way."

"You mean you had to do that every day?" I said.

"That's right," she said. "It got so tough that I finally took Mars out of public school and gave him home teaching every day myself for almost two years during the first and second grade. I used to drive the boys to Tripod and work with Mars while waiting for Cosmo to finish class. Thank goodness Tripod has a program that allows hearing siblings of deaf students to go to school with their deaf brothers and sisters. That's what we eventually did with Mars. And it has worked out wonderfully."

"I'm glad it has worked," I said, "but it sounds a little unorthodox."

"It was," Karen said. "But I'm convinced that parents have to do whatever they must to give their kids an effective education. When we went around to see schools that the other county was offering to us, Cosmo had some aggressive responses. I remember once, we went to a special classroom in our public school district. The teacher who was teaching sign wasn't very good. Cosmo actually grabbed me by the arm to try to pull me out of there. He didn't want any part of that. You might say that he was acting spoiled, but I like to think that he was reacting out of his own frustration, and his desire to communicate."

"Karen, were you frustrated at this point?"

"You bet, Tom. And at that time I was also dealing with some of my own guilt. I felt that I had let Cosmo's development wait too long; I had delayed him because of my own denial. I knew I had to go out and find an answer for my son. We loved the Idyllwild community. The school was perfect for Mars and they were doing a wonderful job teaching him. So before we moved, I tried to solve the problem by taking Cosmo to a normal preschool, and sign-interpret for him myself. But he grabbed my hands and pulled them down, as if to say, 'Don't do that, mommy.'"

"Why did he do that, Karen?" I asked.

"He was overstimulated by everything that was going on around him. I also think he understood that he had to be in a place where sign was the dominant language, not secondary. In this preschool, the kids were communicating verbally. But he was dealing with life on a different level. So it wasn't enough for him to have me sign. Maybe also my sign didn't carry with it nuance—that special feel for language that deaf people express with their sign, that extra artistic flair that makes it special. He knew that his mother's interpreting for him in a standard-language circumstance was wrong. And so we had to move. We had to find Tripod."

"What an experience," I said.

"It was. But the fact that he had responded to me the way he did made me realize that Cosmo needed to be in a situation where the principal language of learning was sign."

"Do you want him to be verbal?" I asked.

"Very much," Arthur said. "But we don't want his intellectual growth hindered by the struggle with language. It's the inevitable crisis in the deaf community, between the American Sign Language people, represented best by Tripod, and on the university level, by Gaullidet in Washington, D.C., and the total communications people who advocate speech. They are best represented by the John Tracy Clinic, here in Los Angeles."

"That's right," Karen said. "And we've never been sorry about our decision. Putting Cosmo in Tripod could not possibly have worked out any better."

"What's the history and the philosophy of Tripod?"

"Well, Tripod was started in 1982 by a mom and dad who were very frustrated," Arthur said, "because when they looked down the road educationally, they couldn't see any opportunities for their hearing-impaired child. They tracked down a fellow named Karl Kirchner, and he became the educational director for what we know today as Tripod. Really, I'd have to say that Tripod was set up as an educational alternative, though now it has become very much a mainstream concept."

"Is the name 'Tripod' significant?" I asked.

"It is, Tom," Karen said. "Back in 1969, Kirchner had written a grant for the government to develop advocacy for parents of deaf and hard-of-hearing children. At that point, there had been no national organization for the deaf, as in the case of the blind and other disabilities. At a national conference held in Washington, D.C., they came up with the Tripod concept. It brought together an educator, a rehabilitation professional, and parents to try to address all of the issues that related to deafness. The meeting was so inspiring that the government continued to write regional grants, and the dream for Tripod's concept was begun. But during the mid-seventies, the federal trough dried up, and there wasn't a way to keep the program alive. What's great though, is that Kirchner never forgot his dream."

"Karl Kirchner may have had a dream for Tripod," I said, "but it didn't happen until after committed parents got involved."

"You're right," Karen said. "Megan Williams has really been the guiding force to create what we now know as Tripod. She's an amazing parent with unbelievable courage and commitment."

"There's nothing like commitment," I said, "and you folks who have children with disabilities have the best reasons to be motivated. Arthur, can you explain the basic tenets of Tripod's philosophy?"

"What makes Tripod different from any other educational program is that it regards parents as parents, not educators. They work to empower our parents to be the best possible, and then those parents trust good professionals to do their jobs. Other programs make the parent the educator. They cop out by saying that if the parent isn't doing his or her job, there's nothing the school can do to help the child with a disability.

"Second, the people at Tripod believe in *total communication.* They're convinced that total communication must dominate the way in which children are taught. And when I say total communication, I mean all of it: an absolute commitment to speech, but a recognition that American Sign Language is the easiest way for the deaf child to learn. You see, in most other school settings, when people talk about this concept, they place the emphasis on speech only. Tripod believes that though verbal communication is important for the growth of a child, it is not as important as his or her intellectual development, and that is furthered best by making sure that the child is comfortable with a form of language he can use.

"They also emphasize an approach that teaches the child to read and write. They make every child literate. They believe that adults who are deaf must interact in the education of children who are deaf. They think that both children who are deaf and their parents need access and interaction with adults who are deaf. Deaf and hard-of-hearing people participate very actively as part of the staff.

"If children who are deaf are going to succeed, they have to have interaction with hearing children. And so, in our parent, infant and preschool levels, hearing children are in the classroom. They are siblings, hearing kids of parents who are deaf, or any other child who interacts with people who are deaf. All the children participate in sign language. And they make sure that the classroom ratio at the beginning is two-thirds hearing impaired to one-third non-impaired. They really believe this concept is critical to the education of a child who is deaf. Still it's difficult to get cities, counties, and states to fund this program, because they see it as 'alternative education,' not mainstream."

"Boy, that's incredible," I said. "I'm blind, and I can tell you that I wish I had had this kind of positive mainstream experience when I was a child. It would have made my life much easier."

"It has done an awful lot for both of our children," Karen said, "and we believe it is the way to educate any child who is disabled."

"What happens after children have had this kind of classroom structure?" I asked.

"We put them into elementary school, away from Tripod. Our model program now is in Burbank, California. We got the Burbank Public School System to reduce their regular class size from thirty hearing kids to twenty. And then we placed eight to ten children who are deaf in the classroom with a second teacher, hearing or deaf, who is trained in the field of deafness. We now have a team-teaching model working very positively using the Tripod concept in Burbank, and we're very excited. This program carries all the way through the middle school years. As the children get older, we continue to change the ratio between deaf and hearing children by adding more and more hearing children. We make sure that both teachers in the classroom are involved in signing so that there's a level of consistency for all of the children involved."

"Arthur, what will happen when Tripod takes this model into high schools?" I asked.

"At that point, we will be changing the ratio back to three-fourths deaf and one-fourth hearing. Tripod believes that the high school work level is so complex, people who are deaf will need more focused teaching time. We want to make sure that our children are involved in normal high school social interactions. That way they won't get isolated."

"It really is a delicate balance to maintain," Karen said. "But Arthur and I have total faith that Tripod will make the right decisions on behalf of all of the children, both deaf and hearing."

"Arthur, is it mostly the question of American Sign Language versus speech that seems to limit the way other schools are dealing with deafness?"

"No. I think that current educational methods just don't work. For years, we've kept developing technologies and machines to do the job. But we really needed to create the right educational *environment* for the children, and then use technology as a supplement to that environment. The Tripod approach of placing hearing and non-hearing children together in the right numbers and with the right support systems is ideal.

"As parents, we find it hard to understand that the system could get so far off course. But I have a slightly different slant on this because I've been a scientist all my life. Science can solve problems until it becomes like the Hydra, the many-headed snake that doubles back on itself, and keeps trying to solve methodologies with methods. That just can't work. And I feel that's what has happened with the education of all children with disabilities."

"I agree with you," I said. "We do have to reduce the issues to basics. It starts by placing young people in settings that allow for their growth, not restricting them with cumbersome bureaucracies, or, to use your phrase, 'complex methodologies.'"

Karen laughed. "Well, I guess you two have just solved all the problems of education that we need on behalf of our children with disabilities, right?"

Now we were all laughing, because we understood that the problem was far more complicated than our answers. Still we felt that we had hit on an important truth. Keep it simple, stupid, I thought. My coaches used to tell me that long ago when I was playing sports. Now, I knew what they meant.

"I understand Tripod's philosophy," I said, "but tell me specifically how Cosmo related to the program."

"It was unbelievable," Karen said. "We had taken Cosmo to programs all around Los Angeles and Orange County. They were teacher-driven programs rather than child-interactive ones. Frankly, Cosmo hated them, and maybe to be fair, he was a discipline problem. But I like to think that instinctively he understood that he could learn more through a sharing process with a combination of good teaching and interaction with other children than he could with the teacher laying down the law. Tripod uses a system very much like Montessori. It's child experiential. Learning isn't programmed, it's experienced. Also Cosmo's first teacher was deaf. She was a marvelous person, and she acted as a significant role model in Cosmo's life. He began to see people who are deaf as successful, interactive human beings, not as creatures isolated by their disability."

Arthur said, "Tripod is involved in an interactive learning experience based on 'reversed mainstreaming.' Non-deaf children are placed in an environment conducive to enlarging the deaf experience, along with the experience of the hearing children."

"Is Tripod still a privately funded program?" I asked.

"It's privately funded," Arthur said, "but it now gets financial support from L.A. Unified Schools. And it has become the deaf center for the Los Angeles school system."

"This has been a remarkable success story," Karen told me. "Arthur Price, the superintendent of schools for the Los Angeles District, just gave a major policy speech in which he pointed to Tripod as the most important new program in the L.A. City Schools."

"Boy, isn't that a breakthrough," I said. "So often school systems feel burdened by kids with disabilities. Now, L.A. Unified says that a child with a disability is bringing something wonderful to the system. I think that's just great.

"Arthur, I've been asking the families I've interviewed to tell me about the interaction between the child with the disability and the other siblings in the family. So talk to me about Mars and Cosmo. How do they feel about each other?"

"It has been interesting to observe, Tom, especially during the early years. Cosmo is forceful and self-assertive, and he has always been so much smaller than Mars. It was really a blessing that he had an older brother to contend with. Cosmo has so much energy, he needs to have a sibling who will challenge him and, in some ways, control him. They used to fight, physically, and sometimes Cosmo would win. I think that Mars let him. But they've been able to find a balance and provide Cosmo with the kind of outlet he needs."

"Karen, I suppose Mars could have said, 'I don't want any part of this brother with a disability.'"

"To be honest," Karen told me, "he did. Mars will still say that the worst day of his life was when Cosmo was born. He has had a hard time accepting Cosmo's deafness. Until Mars came to Tripod and became interactive with deafness, I was worried. But again, Tripod made the difference, not just in the way Mars dealt with his brother but in softening his edges and providing him with a sense of interaction with many people. You see, because of his brilliance, he has his own special needs, since he's always perceived as different. So when he was involved in Tripod, he learned that 'difference' can be turned into 'wonderful.' I think that helped him grow a lot."

Arthur said, "In practical terms, a big part of the breakthrough occurred when the boys learned American Sign Language. They no longer had to resort to fighting to communicate. That's a strong argument for the ASL System being taught to non-deaf kids."

"Arthur, now that the boys can communicate, how would you say they handle each other?"

"Very well," Arthur said. "I've gotten us all involved in family projects around this house, from putting on a new roof, to remodeling. I like to do that, and thank goodness, I have a couple of sons who want to share it with me. Even though Cosmo is only eight and deaf, he digs right in. Last weekend, as we were putting on the new roof, I made the boys work in the buddy system, as a production team. They did remarkably well. It was great to see them like that.

"Under the Americans With Disabilities Act and the Child Rights Act, children are guaranteed that they can attend the least-restrictive educational environment. But that's like saying, 'Give them the environment where they get the least,' because they're lumped in with so many other kids who aren't relating in any way to their disability. When I watch Mars and Cosmo, I see two boys who have become interactive and are not making more of the disability than it should be. We're beginning to see the change from disability to ability in Cosmo. A big part of that comes from the fact that Tripod meets his special needs, and he communicates easily with his most important peer, Mars."

"There's a parent group called 'Impact High,'" Karen added. "It was started by Ginger Greeves, the woman who first turned us on to Tripod. This group seeks to provide the child with the least-restrictive environment, while guaranteeing his or her access to total communication. By adding in the communications criteria, the children are now moving around L.A. Unified effectively and gaining the educational elements that they need to grow. Unfortunately, each SELPA in the system is still trying to offer programs for every disability because their charter requires the 'least-restrictive environment.' Consequently, resources are tremendously misused."

Arthur was animated now. "We've just got to get rid of this idea that many programs are better than a few programs that can bring major quality to the system. Two or three concepts like Tripod in an area even the size of Southern California would be enough. I think Tripod is creating a precedent that will be carried into the twenty-first century."

"I certainly hope so," I said.

Karen said, "I've gotten involved in a Tripod hotline, which answers questions of parents all around the country. I've found that there are incredible levels of anxiety, because the parents of children who are deaf are simply not getting the right information."

"What do they talk about?" I asked.

"It could be anything, from asking about total communication, to talking about sibling rivalry questions, to simple things such as what kind of hearing aids are best. And then we also face issues that are tremendously complicated. Sometimes people need help coping with divorce. As you know, Tom, divorce is a major issue when dealing with parents of children who are disabled. Some parents tell me they can't handle their child's deafness, and they feel they need to place the child in a foster home. I hate it when I get those calls."

"I have a friend who went through that experience when she was a little girl," I said. "She's very open about telling me, and all of her friends who are deaf, that she has never gotten over the trauma."

"Besides parenting my kids, the parent hotline is my most important job," Karen said. "It's my way of giving back, based on what Tripod has given us. I am constantly amazed at how many parents are misinformed. We've all got a long way to go."

"Arthur, I know you've both learned American Sign Language. But I've heard from people who know how to sign that just as a deaf person may be uncomfortable with trying to make speech work as a part of their lives, a non-deaf person's sign language isn't very good."

They both laughed.

"You're right about that. There are times when Cosmo purposely talks to us in very slow sign language, with great exaggeration, as if he's trying to tell us that he thinks we're not only slow, but retarded. It's amazing to see him do this. It makes us aware of how inadequate we are, and I suppose it makes us understand how complex this issue of communications really is."

"What about Cosmo's interaction with other children who have not been exposed to hearing-impaired kids?" I asked. "How does he do?"

"Somehow he seems to survive," Arthur said. "He has tremendous courage. The other day he left the house and wandered down to the corner grocery with some money he had been given for his birthday. Without being able to communicate, he was still able to buy exactly what he wanted, bring it home, and enjoy it. He has a little friend next door. I know that this boy has no knowledge of American Sign Language, yet, they play games and seem to communicate easily. Maybe this is one of those special gifts of children who are disabled. I find it absolutely remarkable."

Karen said, "We don't want to gloss over this issue, Tom. We know that it's not going to be easy for Cosmo to find his place with children who aren't hearing-impaired exposed. But at eight years old, he seems to have the instinct necessary to allow him to find the path of least resistance and communicate. I don't mean that he can communicate complex philosophy or ideas that call for elaboration. But he finds ways to get his basic needs met.

"When you first came in today, you met our friend Thomas from Australia, who's living with us now. His son, Luke, is the same age as Mars, and it has been interesting to watch Cosmo find his place with these two boys. Cosmo has to be more cooperative than he used to be, because Mars has an alternative playmate. I'll give you an example: Cosmo used to scream to get our attention. He knew he couldn't hear himself scream, and that it didn't bother him—it only bothered us. He'd keep it up until he got our full attention. Now that's not working because Luke and Mars simply go off and play together. Cosmo's lost one of his levers, and he's had to learn to communicate with all of us on a different level."

Arthur asked, "Tom, when you were a little boy, how do you think your mother perceived your blindness?"

"That's a complex question," I said. "They didn't think I would be limited, but they had no conception my life would be as full as it is."

"I'm interested to hear that," Arthur said, "because we feel just the opposite. We are astounded every day at what Cosmo is achieving. We expect him to be able to do all the things that he chooses in life. Is that being optimistic? Maybe it is. But I think there's precedent for it. All over the world, deaf people are beating the odds and making major contributions to their societies. Are they still a minority? Yes, that's true. Is deafness still the most isolating of all disabilities? I think it is. But when you've been through a system like Tripod, you come to believe that success is possible, and you start to commit yourself to the idea that it's important to think about what your child will be, rather than what he will not achieve.

"In our case, we know that Cosmo is being raised in a loving home by people committed, not only to his welfare but to support his dreams. We also know that we have been very lucky to find a program like Tripod that enlarges our understanding of what's possible for Cosmo, and Cosmo's sense of his own self-worth. For us, the parent puzzle has all the pieces in the right places at this point."

"Are you worried about his teenage years?" I asked. "Or where he may go to college, and what he might do as a professional?"

"Of course we are," Karen said. "But isn't any parent with any child? We have learned to deal with Cosmo's deafness as only one part of who he is. Every day we work to make that element less significant, and we celebrate his uniqueness and enjoy all of his achievements."

"You know," I said, "there's no way I can add any more to what you've told me. I really appreciate the time we've shared, and I'm grateful that you've opened up my ears to the unlimited possibilities of the spirit found within a child who is deaf, and supported by parents and a system that works."

CHAPTER

Cheri and David

I LOVE IT WHEN opportunity and purpose come together in a way that can only be called serendipity. Whether you believe that God's hand touches circumstance, or that fate rules our destiny, when people are brought together by accident, and exciting results occur, it can be one of the most unique experiences in life.

That's exactly how I felt when I met Cheri and David Hartman, while both David and I were receiving an award in upstate New York.

David Hartman and I are both blind, but that is not why I chose to add the Hartman family to this work. They are also remarkable people. David is a practicing psychiatrist, and Cheri has a doctorate in educational psychology. Their place in this work becomes obvious when you hear the story of Jeanie Hartman, their nine-year-old daughter who is dealing with Attention Deficit Disorder, a complex learning issue that we are just beginning to understand.

Because of everybody's busy schedule, our phone calls were conducted at six o'clock in the morning, California time, with Dr. Cheri Hartman, and late into the evening with Dr. David Hartman. So with a cup of coffee and my tape recorder, I began by asking Cheri, as I often have in this book, if the pregnancies of her three children, Doug, Paul, and Jeanie, had been normal.

"Completely, Tom. No problems at all. The boys came into the world as if they thought it would be their oyster."

"And Jeanie?" I asked.

"She was just fine," Cheri said. "In fact, when I was in the delivery room, David used hypnotic suggestion on me, and I just breezed through her birth."

"When Jeanie was born, the boys were in school, right?"

"Just about," Cheri told me. "Doug was in first grade and Paul was starting preschool, so it was busy around the Hartman house."

"Was David a helpful parent?" I asked.

"Very much. But I've always been the principal Parent Advocate. David likes to look at the big picture, and he's very slow to make decisions, not because he's indecisive but because he's extremely careful. I suppose it goes with his profession. I think our family has been well served by our different personalities."

"How about the boys, Cheri. Are they different?"

"Oh yes. Doug has always been the archetype of a big brother. He has been one of those boys who comes off like a little man, right from the beginning—very serious and organized. David tells me that Paul is very much a middle child. He's in awe of his brother, yet wants to be more adventurous than Doug. I think he's jealous of his little sister. I know he believes she gets much too much attention."

"That doesn't sound odd for a family," I said. "It's just that in your case, Jeanie's issues make the circumstances a little more intense. Right?"

"That's true. We try to give everyone equal amounts of attention, but I'm sure Jeanie gets a bigger dose. David is great at his investment of weekend quality time with the children. And, thank goodness, he's better at math than I am. When the boys have a problem in that area, I send them to the other Dr. Hartman."

"Boy, Cheri, I can relate to this. When our children were growing up, I got all their book reports to do, and Patty worked on the math side because I failed algebra, twice. But to get back to Jeanie, she was born with no real complications. Did the learning disability manifest itself early?"

"No, it didn't. We did have a very early scare, though. From the time Jeanie was six months old until she was eighteen months, she just stopped growing. Her appetite was smaller than the boys' had been, and her language skills were somewhat delayed compared to theirs. I began to really get worried. So we had her tested for every possible horrible disease that the doctors could think of. None of the tests came up with any findings."

"Then when did you begin to suspect that Jeanie might have a problem?" I asked.

"Well, I knew early on that she might be developmentally delayed, but I didn't find that unusual. It happens to many children. I wonder now if this was one of those times when being a mother and also being a professional are in conflict. The professional, in this case, rationalized for the mother. I said, 'Maybe Jeanie's developmentally delayed, but I've seen many children with delays catch up, so there isn't a reason to over-react.' The mother, on the other hand, was saying, 'I'd better get to work and pay close attention to the possibility of a problem for my child.' Human beings are weird composites of a lot of things, aren't we?"

"No question about that," I said. "So you really didn't pick up on Jeanie's issues until you got her into preschool, right?"

"Even though we believed it was quite likely that Jeanie had a disability, it would have been inappropriate to identify Jeanie as having a problem at that time. By the way, I want to correct something we said earlier. We were talking about the boys, and I told you that when Jeanie was born, she got much more attention than they did. Probably in physical terms, and maybe even emotionally that's true. But she was a third child, and because the boys were older, I was constantly dragging her around in the car, keeping up with their schedule. I accepted certain behaviors that I would never have allowed, particularly with Doug."

"What do you mean?" I asked.

"Well, she ate food that wasn't the best for her, she watched a lot of television, some of it not so healthy, and she heard language all the time that was above her head, because our conversations were with the boys, not specifically with her. When you deal with three children, you probably become a little more insensitive to specific issues, since you're trying to achieve—and I'm not proud to say this—the generalities of child rearing. So I think that I was stretched a little thin. And then there was that rationalization ability. I could come up with an educated answer for the delays I saw in my daughter. It's also amazing, now that I think about it, that I had a sister who was learning disabled. I was totally involved in her life, teaching her to read, when she was a little girl. Yet when it came to Jeanie, I was as late as any parent picking up on the cues."

"Cheri, was this because there's a lot of gray area in diagnosis?"

"Tom, here's the Dr. Cheri Hartman theory about learning disability. Jeanie deals with a disability defined as Attention Deficit Disorder, ADD. That's not necessarily what we call learning disability. Actually, some doctors refer to the disability as ADHD, Attention Deficit Hyperactivity Disorder. But I like to think of it as just ADD.

"I believe that a learning disability connects directly to

biology and genetics. A child who, for whatever reason, is developmentally delayed may or may not have a learning disability. Many children who have a biological delay do not have learning disability, and yet many do. Those disabilities manifest themselves in specific educational issues, such as understanding the connection between letters and words, and being able to frame the sequencing of numbers. Many of the things that we measure academic standards by fall within the parameters of learning disability.

"These children do not seem to have the capacity to hold back on expressing impulses. They can be moody, I think largely because of low self-esteem. Sometimes they seek comfort from peer relationships by playing with younger children and regressing to earlier periods of behavior, sometimes even to toddlerhood. They may struggle with developing positive self-images.

"Professionals, like David and me, believe that Attention Deficit Disorder also has a basis in brain chemistry. That's why children with this issue are treated with Ritalin. It seems to control the impulsive behavior and allow them to learn on a more appropriate educational track.

"This whole business is very complicated for parents, because in the school system, you must know where your child fits in order to get the right classroom participation. Attention Deficit Disorder is very different from just a learning disability, though they both may be found in a child, or can function as independent parts in the child. For years, people who tested children and developed Individual Education Plans have struggled with the delineation of these issues. And it becomes of paramount importance for the parent to be able to sort them out."

"So Cheri, when did you and David finally begin to confront this issue?"

"Well, Tom, when Jeanie was three, she went to a preschool,

and I think this was where the problem began to manifest itself. Her teacher was totally inappropriate. She thought of Jeanie as a problem child. The term she used often was 'behaviorly inappropriate.' And I couldn't see that at all. There are many three-year-olds in preschool who are not task-orientated, and Jeanie just would not carry out tasks. She became a major personality problem for this teacher, and I probably wasn't quick enough to respond to the issue."

"Cheri, I think you're being too hard on yourself, because I know from my own experience that children with learning disabilities can demonstrate appropriate behavior when they are at home."

"That's true. And I probably became defensive about Jeanie and this teacher, so I tended to mask the problem. But I also was pulling that rationalization act again. I thought, 'If Jeanie is developmentally delayed, we'll create such a loving environment for her here at home that she'll catch up. I know that I can find the right supports to facilitate her education.'"

"So it's fair to say that preschool was a disaster, but you pushed on to kindergarten?"

"Not right away. We knew that Jeanie had what I perceived as delay problems, so we held her back a year."

"Did that help?"

"Not really. I can't say that kindergarten got much better. I should expand on this. At this point, neither Dr. David Hartman, psychiatrist, or Dr. Cheri Hartman, educational psychologist, had decided that Jeanie had a learning disability. We still were hoping, and I know that word is true, hoping, that what we were facing was just an issue of delay, not of learning disability."

"Cheri, talk about the symptoms that can cause these kinds of parental confusions."

"It was very clear that going into kindergarten, Jeanie had a short-term memory problem. We had spent a lot of time over the summer trying to help her learn her ABCs, and how to count. These are both memory activities necessary for fulfilling school requirements. Since Jeanie was finding these concepts difficult, I started to get an inkling that we had a problem. Remember, we had kept her back, so by now she was six years old. I had to face the fact that she might not outgrow this kind of difficulty, and that a learning issue might be involved."

"Was this then still a question of denial?"

"I don't think so, but then again there must have been a certain level of denial on my part, and I think on David's."

"What do you mean?" I asked.

"As the ultimate optimist and a professional educator, I was sure that we could handle any problems that might come up within Jeanie's education. I really didn't think that we'd have to go through any personal agony. I was sure that between David and me, we had the professional talents to cope."

"There was good reason for you to feel that way," I said.

"I suppose so, Tom. But it probably was a sense of overconfidence."

"Well, okay. I'll accept that for now. But I really think it was more a question of being able to believe in yourselves enough to know that you could deal with the issues of your children, and I don't think that's unusual. At any rate, take me through the kindergarten experience."

"What happened that year was surprising to me. The teacher placed a lot of pressure on us to get Jeanie to the same point as the other kids in the class. This teacher was an intense person but very dedicated. Apparently, Jeanie had difficulty learning abstract word and memory tasks. She was having trouble with very simple numbers, and, I have to say, Jeanie was having a great deal of trouble with attention in general. There were behaviors that I know had to be categorized as distractions in the school setting. For example, she is a very affectionate child; in the classroom, she would inappropriately start hugging a classmate or even the teacher. She was demonstrating what we've come to understand as Attention Deficit Disorder, but at the time, the teacher felt that it was simply a behavioral difficulty. In girls, Attention Deficit Disorder behavior is usually very difficult to categorize. Most of the time, girls manifest this quite differently from boys. Boys' behavior is much more aggressive, so schools tend to take it more seriously while girls are overly affectionate and inappropriately loving."

I said, " I guess there is a lot of gray area in ADD."

"That's right, Tom. We were a couple of months into the year before the teacher started to give me feedback. In retrospect, I think she was confused because she knew Jeanie came from a well-educated family. David and I were both professionals in related fields, so she was probably hesitant to voice her feelings. I really don't blame her for that."

"Cheri, when was the concept of Attention Deficit Disorder introduced in the conversations about Jeanie?"

"I think I actually introduced it during a parent/teacher conference. The situation at school had deteriorated to a point where Jeanie didn't want to even go to school. I think she fell into a serious depression. It was very noticeable to all of us that her moods were way down."

"Was there a red flag for David at this point?"

"David came to the conference with me, and I honestly think that he was reluctant to see Jeanie as learning disabled. He has been this way with all the kids; he doesn't like to put labels on any form of behavior. I, on the other hand, have been much more aggressive at suggesting professional help. I don't know if David was in denial, or whether it related specifically to his sense of fairness when it came to disability, but in the meeting with Jeanie's teacher, we did talk about the issue. I really wanted this conference. As I look back now, I wanted to talk with Jeanie's teacher, not because I had scientific data supporting the thought that Jeanie had a learning disability but because I was functioning as a mother. I felt that there had to be an intervention on behalf of my child. Had Jeanie had a different kind of kindergarten teacher, I might not even have picked up on all of this.

"When Jeanie was in preschool, she wanted attention. Even though her classroom teacher perceived her as a behavioral problem, everyone else thought of her as a loving child. She was the star of her preschool. I laugh now because she was the child that people wanted to love. I remember David and I going to her school play. She had the lead role. But when she got to kindergarten and the work became structurally task-based, she struggled. Her friendliness was no longer paying off. And so we had to have this conference."

"So, Cheri, you went to the conference with a lot of apprehension and the beginnings of frustration. What did you talk about with this teacher?"

"First of all, I was upset because the teacher had made a decision that Jeanie was a behavioral problem. She had actually yelled at her in class. Now, to little Jeanie Hartman, this was devastating. David believes that Jeanie was on the edge of a clinical depression. We really had to drag her to school every day. These patterns of behaviors just weren't right. So I had decided that whether or not her classroom behavior was part of a learning disability, I was sure we had to get them under control. We were at a serious impasse, and we had to effectively identify Jeanie's problem. I knew this would get the kindergarten teacher off the hook, because she could say, 'Wow, she's got a learning disability, and it's not my fault.' So, that's what she needed. Out of that conference, we agreed to have Jeanie tested.

"In the life of every parent, there are moments that stand out as turning points in the relationship, and we clearly had one with Jeanie. It was right around Thanksgiving. School had ended for the day, but I had to go back to pick up Paul. Jeanie saw her teacher coming out of the door of the school, and she actually flattened out on the floor of the car and burst into tears. She kept saying, 'Don't let her see me, don't let her see me.' I was so startled. I'd never had a child act like that toward a teacher."

"Did it make you angry that a teacher could affect your child that much?"

"I was not angry, Tom, but I was horrified at Jeanie's reaction and at my own lack of awareness. Looking back now, I'm glad that all of this happened, because I might have gone on quite a while without becoming proactive on Jeanie's behalf. When she had this reaction toward her teacher, I knew I had to do something. And so, when we had the conference, I pressed for the testing."

"Cheri, how did the school react to this?"

"Schools vary a great deal in the approach they take toward parent intervention. Jeanie's principal and her predecessor believed that parental intervention could only make their jobs more difficult. The atmosphere was not conducive for me to get involved on Jeanie's behalf. The principal is a woman who gets along well with the children, even Jeanie, but is extremely confrontational with parents. I think it probably comes from some level of insecurity, at least that's what I think Dr. David would say. But it's very difficult to operate in that circumstance."

"Cheri, let me understand. You agreed to the testing during the meeting."

"I could see the stress go out of Jeanie's teacher's face when we suggested testing. For her, Jeanie Hartman had just become too much. She wanted the problem identified. She was a very fine teacher, but systems and personality needs can get into some horrible collisions on the educational highway, and that's what happened to Jeanie."

"There's an important lesson for parents in this, Cheri, because you didn't lose it. You found a way to work with this teacher."

"I did, Tom. The minute we agreed to the testing, and I got her to allow Jeanie to work at her own pace, their relationship improved tremendously. We had a problem at this point though, and weren't able to test Jeanie until March of her kindergarten year."

"Why was that?" I asked.

"Well, she got quite ill. She developed chicken pox in January, which led to a virus that completely immobilized her body. To all the doctors it looked as if she had lupus. All of her joints were frozen and she was in tremendous pain. For about a week, she couldn't even walk. This was a horrible time for all of us.

"I believed I could handle the educational and learning issues, but this was something physical. David was frustrated because none of the doctors could come up with a reasonable diagnosis, just like when Jeanie was eighteen months old. We still don't know what it was.

"I remember a day that was awful. She was on the couch, and I couldn't wake her up. She totally shut down. It was in the middle of the afternoon and I was home alone with her, so I put her in the car and rushed her to the doctor. By the time I'd gotten there, she woke up. Her body must have shut down to heal itself, because, amazingly, she felt better than she had in months. It clearly pointed out my sense of inadequacy. No matter what one's educational background, every parent faces moments with their children that they just cannot handle. And this was one of those times. I was so grateful I hadn't taken a job, because I wouldn't have been around for Jeanie."

"I'll tell you, Cheri, we're back to this concept of fate again."

"I believe that, Tom. And I believe I was meant to stay home with Jeanie."

"Were there any lasting physical issues that came out of this unknown virus?"

"Jeanie went through a series of difficult tests that led the doctors to believe that she could be developing complex lupus disease. It turns out now that it was symptomatic, and she has not acquired an active disease. They do say that it could be an issue in later life, but for now, she's physically fine. Those were horrible months for us, particularly for David. He had put his faith in medicine, and now his colleagues couldn't come up with appropriate answers."

"So, Cheri, it was March before you took Jeanie to a professional tester."

"Yes. We took her to the best professional we could find to give her a battery of psychometric tests. These are eye-hand coordination tests that indicate certain learning disabilities."

"Was Jeanie frustrated during these tests?" I asked.

"No, not really. The professional tester, a doctor, did a wonderful job putting her at ease. She made Jeanie think that she was playing games. That's a special gift in itself."

"Now, Cheri, I'd say that's a qualified response to my question. You liked the way she did the test, but you're not necessarily impressed with her?"

I could hear Cheri's laughter coming down the phone wire.

"Look, Cheri," I said, "Hartman's not the only smart blind guy around here. He doesn't have that sensitivity stuff bottled. I've got a few of those skills."

"Well, Tom, my reservations about the doctor is that when she gives the test results to parents, she's much too technical. Here's a sample of what she wrote: 'Early motoric and language skills were met within normal time intervals. Jeanie was retained in the three-year-old preschool program due to immaturity, both in the classroom and in the hierarchy of peer group social interaction.' The mumbo jumbo goes on from there.

"Because I am an educational specialist, this stuff didn't

sound like mumbo jumbo to me. I'd read the reports and say, 'Wow, yeah, I understand.' But my psychiatrist husband was listening to this and saying, 'All right, Cheri, translate for me,' and he's a doctor. What happens to parents without our backgrounds, when they're subjected to these kinds of test reports? They pay hundreds of dollars for these assessments and go home saying to each other, 'What do these tell us?'"

"Well, Dr. Hartman, you went home with Dr. Hartman and evaluated the report as a professional and as a parent. What did it tell you?"

"For us, it did confirm that Jeanie had both a learning disability and Attention Deficit Disorder. Let me see if I can find the section in the report that clearly defines her opinion. Oh, here it is: 'Social function in a group environment is difficult for Jeanie. She is struggling with her classmates currently, because she is seeking their attention through inappropriate means. She shows distress in the classroom, with a tendency to pick at herself until she bleeds. She sometimes cannot leave her classmates alone, even when they're involved in goal-related activities. She's aware when she's being rejected, and says that it's difficult for her to make new friends. She states she wants her own way and tells me that she does not like school.

"'My conclusions and recommendations are these: developmentally, Jeanie has a very uneven profile, and presents a classic learning-disabled child, with prominent symptoms of developmental reading disorder and Attention Deficit Hyperactivity Disorder. Verbal comprehension skills are average. Visual and auditory perceptual skills, memory function and attentiveness are poor.' Her recommendation was tutoring and enrollment in a school called The Achievement Center.

"This was when my intuitions were confirmed. The Achievement Center is a private school for learning-disabled children. I had high hopes that in this educational setting, Jeanie would be just fine. Still, the fact that the doctor recommended this school shattered any hopes I might have had that we were dealing with just delay.

"As I was going through these papers, I just found a parent handbook that indicates the symptoms of Attention Deficit Disorder. This supports what I was saying about explaining a problem appropriately to parents versus confusing them with psychological mumbo jumbo. Here's the simplest language that describes the condition:

"'Kids with Attention Deficit Hyperactivity Disorder may have some or all of the following problems: they may have trouble paying attention, they may have trouble thinking before acting, and their behavior can be characterized as totally impulsive. Parents should not be frightened at the use of Ritalin, a drug that has had remarkable success in the treatment of these children.'

"This little handbook went on to point out that the attention deficit manifests itself differently in girls and boys. 'In girls,' and I'm quoting from the book again, 'it causes the need for affection and a constant sense of fears that are usually unfounded. Loud noises can send these children into great levels of panic, and some of the children may have a profound phobia about insects, particularly bees. For some reason, this bee phobia is common to little girls with Attention Deficit Disorder.' And that was true for Jeanie."

"That's fascinating," I said. "You were able to gain this information so much easier in a well-written handbook than you could from a complex clinical report?"

"You bet, Tom."

"So the recommendation was that Jeanie should go to The Achievement Center. How did you feel about that?"

"I was actually excited because I'd heard great things about The Achievement Center from friends in the learning business. It's funny. When I thought of myself going back to work, I often pictured myself as a reading specialist, happily helping children in The Achievement Center. So it was a big shock when I visited the classrooms and saw the curriculum."

"Why was it a shock?"

"The teaching methods were so outdated, I couldn't even comprehend that they were being used in a private educational program. This was so shattering because I had decided—with that optimistic mentality of mine—that once I diagnosed a problem and searched out the best solution, everything would be fine. I was devastated when I saw this system."

"Cheri, can you explain what was wrong?"

"Tom, I'd had extended training as a reading specialist, and I saw a teacher using a method my professors at Temple University said would set children back years and could only be described as damaging. If you were teaching a child to read the word 'cat,' under this antiquated method, you would take each letter and attach a sound to it. So you say, 'cuh-ah-t, cat.' I'm sure that I even blanched and I tried to catch myself so no one would see. I decided that maybe the teacher was just using this method on only one child. I listened and watched a little longer. The teacher moved on to another student, who was able to identify the entire word, but she still made him sound it out letter by letter. I was horrified.

"I walked outside and broke down. When I pulled myself together, I went to the library to see what literature the teachers were working from. Amazingly, they had all the contemporary literature necessary, yet teachers weren't keeping current.

"So I said to the administrators, 'How can you not have your people reading the appropriate material?' They shrugged it off as unimportant. Tom, I was crazed. I went home and told David that there was no way Jeanie was going to that school."

"What was your alternative?"

"The public school. But unlike so many parents, we got lucky. Thank goodness we did. I'm not somebody who cries a lot, but during those days, while we were searching for an alternative program, I kept breaking down. I'm so grateful that David is such a rock. He didn't ever lose focus of the goal. He has that internalized determination that must come from having had to cope with monumental problems all of his life. I think guys like you and David are unique in that way."

"I don't know, Cheri. We crumble sometimes. At any rate, after your disappointment, you moved on to look at the public school?"

"Actually, we did look at another private possibility and it was worse."

"So you're zero for two. What's left is the public school."

"That's right. But I want to make a point here. Had parents who were not professional educators gone to see The Achievement Center, they would have looked at these classrooms with small numbers of kids and attentive teachers and placed their children there without a second thought. Had I not been a specialist, I don't know that I would have picked up on how outdated the methods were."

"Cheri, you're not making the parents who read this text feel any better."

"I know that, but there is a correlation here that I think can help all parents who deal with children with disability. I didn't like any of the teachers I saw until we came to the public school. Parents may not have professional skills like I do, but they have a lifetime of cultivated instinct, and I think they need to trust that instinct. It can carry them a lot further than any Ph.D."

"That's what I've found in talking to other parents. They seem to be able to sense the needs of their children better than anyone else. And need is answered first and foremost by good people with commitment to children. Let's hope that all parents have a chance to find solid individuals who touch the lives of their children. So you moved on to the public school?"

"As you know, many parents have a negative perception of

what's available in public education. Even though I had a professional background, I have to admit I felt the way most parents do. I believed that schools were overcrowded, and that the systems were not individualized. I believed that the teachers were overburdened. I was delighted to find out that I was wrong. Still, I don't want to give the impression it was easy. There was a grocery list of things to do. I talked to the principal of the public school and asked who I should call to get the process started.

"The principal said, 'I think you should call Bob Sief, the Director of Special Education for the city.' This guy was great. It was wonderful to meet an administrator who was sensitive to an individual child's needs. After my meeting with Dr. Sief, I continued to call him through the summer, making sure that he would help Jeanie complete a second, extended battery of tests required for her to go to public school. These tests were far more oriented toward finding a way for Jeanie to work effectively in a classroom system. The tests were much more focused on helping us understand Jeanie's strengths and weaknesses, rather than just trying to pigeonhole her. I also asked Dr. Sief to help me select an appropriate classroom teacher for Jeanie."

"Cheri, what classroom recommendation did they make for her?"

"All the professionals believed that Jeanie Hartman clearly needed to be in an effective resource room, but she would have to go through an eligibility process. This guarantees that students can gain access to appropriate services."

"You know, Cheri, throughout the book, parents have talked about qualifying their kids to fit in certain niches."

"That's right. In our case, Jeanie had to go through the extensive battery of tests I noted before, to define this eligibility, and to be on the drug Ritalin—which helps her with her Attention Deficit Disorder. She also needed ongoing, appropriate clinical evaluations to help define the balance between the hours spent in a necessary resource room, and the normal classes she would take with other children. I know that many parents fear having their children labeled, and most of them hate the IEP Process. But I have come to see with the teenagers I work with now that for the ones who have fallen through the cracks—it's a double-edged sword. On the one hand, you don't want children labeled. On the other hand, if you properly diagnose the problem at the beginning of the educational process, the learning can be geared in a positive direction on behalf of the child. So I believe parents have to keep trying to use the system appropriately, even when they're frustrated."

"That's great advice, Cheri. I hadn't heard it put quite that way."

"I want to go back, to explain how thorough this testing process was, even though it was somewhat frightening. There were five parts. First, they did an educational assessment. That was followed by a socio-cultural assessment given by a team of professionals who come and do parent interviews and go through a special behavioral checklist. Some parents feel as if they're being scrutinized at this point, and become afraid. But this is useful, because the team wants to understand your child's background and how she adapts to the school. The third component is the medical evaluation. Then there's the general psychological testing profile. We were able to avoid that test because we had just gone through it the year before. Finally, the fifth group of tests are standard speech and language evaluations. Communication is so important. We have to know where the kids are when it comes to these critical tools.

"Once all of these tests were completed, we were able to make the IEP work for us. Even though the language of the IEP is confusing to most parents, we found ways to use the information effectively to select the right school and the right resource teacher for Jeanie. She has had this teacher for two years now, and she absolutely loves her.

"As a result of this process, we saw the Child Rights Act [the law that we call '94–142'] work in a very positive way. It guarantees that all children will have access to learning resources deemed appropriate for their education. If you can read the language of the IEP, and get people to comply, you can really get a lot done.

"At this point, I'm satisfied with Jeanie's education. I do think she might be able to move a little quicker, but she's happy with her educational environment, she loves her teacher, Debbie Jones. I think she's also beginning to feel socially more adequate.

"There are those times when I still need to tweak the system, here in Virginia. We have a state law titled 'Parental Rights in Special Education' that we rely on to understand our rights. Unfortunately, it is written in a language I call 'Educationese,' not English. It's confusing for parents who don't have my background. For example, the public school is called 'LEA.' That's Local Educational Agency. Why can't they just say school? They don't tell parents what 'LEA' means, so if they read it, they'd think it's another bureaucracy. Also, even if you understand your parent-rights document, that doesn't mean you're going to be able to sort through the system, to find out who you're supposed to deal with. That's a whole other issue. And that speaks to a question of parents being willing to fight the battle all the way, to advocate themselves right to the top, and, if necessary, to use the law on behalf of their child. I do believe that if you can ask the right questions, you can get the system to work for you. And over the last couple of years, I've learned how to ask the right questions."

"Cheri, I think that's important for all parents, this idea of learning to ask the right questions. What might be the most important question that parents ought to ask on behalf of their child?"

"I think it has to do with knowing the classroom circumstance your child is going to be in. What kind of resource room is going to be made available for the child you love."

"Was that your concern when Jeanie was going to the first grade?"

"Yes, Tom. In many resource rooms around the country, kids with learning disabilities can be lumped together with children who are emotionally disturbed. I was concerned that Jeanie was going to be in a room with kids who fight or even bite. Some other parents who I talked to made me nervous because their children had this experience. In our case, the public school has an excellent designation separating kids who are emotionally disturbed from kids with learning disabilities."

"When you first saw your public school, did you feel good about it immediately?"

"I did. It's important for parents to have a feeling, in terms of what they might be looking for, when they judge their school setting. I saw eclecticism, combined with multiple sensory modalities. I saw appropriate use of phonics with effective recognition, provided for both children with learning disabilities and children with Attention Deficit Disorder."

I was laughing now. "Cheri, you're starting to sound like those technical people you told me about."

"I'm sorry, Tom." Cheri was joining me in the laughter. "It's my background. It comes through every once in a while. The point is, parents should be looking for a circumstance in which their children are given a full cross-section of learning experiences. They want to feel as if the system their child is in is doing everything possible to tap into his or her potential."

"You talked about Jeanie having the right teacher in the public schools. What quality means the most to you when evaluating a teacher for any child with a disability?"

"The most important quality is love. Debbie Jones, Jeanie's teacher in the first and second grade resource room, overflows with love. She makes every child feel that he or she is important. After Jeanie Hartman's kindergarten experience, that has been critical."

"Cheri, I know a lot of parents wonder how they should deal with the use of Ritalin for Attention Deficit Disorder. How did you work out an effective protocol between Jeanie's doctor and her teacher in defining her use of this drug."

"At the beginning of the school year, I asked Debbie Jones, the teacher, to assess when Jeanie might start using Ritalin. Debbie felt that we should wait a couple of weeks to see how Jeanie would do without it. That was a good approach. The theory was, 'Let's see how much she can learn, and then move the dosage up as necessary on a gradual basis.' She believed that sometimes a new environment, like Jeanie's school, with small, focused classrooms and small numbers of students, can be very helpful with children like Jeanie. David agreed with this concept, because that's the approach he takes in his own practice when sorting out the effective use of medications. Debbie Jones also talked to Jeanie's teachers in her mainstream classes, to get a sense of her behavior.

"After about a month, we came to the collective decision that Ritalin would be appropriate. We started her on five milligrams twice a day, and the improvement was very marked. We did notice, however, that toward the end of Jeanie's day, she experienced significant mood swings and behavioral problems. With the doctor's guidance, and helpful consultation among Debbie Jones and Jeanie's other teachers, she is now on a more effective protocol. It's called twenty milligrams slow release. Sometimes when you put children on this Ritalin format, they stop eating and maybe don't sleep regularly, but Jeanie has thrived, and we are just delighted. The changes have been incredible.

"But I don't want to give the impression that we think Ritalin is the only solution. It's just part of it. In fact, during the summer, we took Jeanie off the drug because she wasn't in a stressful environment. We allowed her to, I guess you'd say, detox. I think that's a good idea for parents. When she went back to school for the second grade, she experienced a month of adjustment; she returned to the protocol with some mood swings. But I'd rather deal with that, and give her occasional breaks from her medicine, than keep her on the drug full-time.

"No one fully understands the relationship in ADD between the chemical imbalance in the brain, and social pressures brought on from the outside. As a parent, I'm trying to make intelligent decisions as we go along. Ritalin does bring out the best in Jeanie in a school setting. Some parents fear that drugs alter the real child, but it helps Jeanie be the child that she wants to be. The impact on her self-concept has been marvelously positive."

"Cheri, it sounds to me like you're making great decisions."

"Well, I've got the right partner to make them with. He has a special feel, not just for the medical questions but also for the social ones."

"Let's talk about that," I said. "Tell me about how Jeanie does with her peer group."

"This has been one of my remaining concerns when I talk about Jeanie being mainstreamed in the public school. I worry about how she's going to do, not just in school but with the same kids as she develops friendships in her neighborhood environment. Up to now, it hasn't been a big problem, because my neighbors have been very sensitive about not letting their kids view Jeanie in any kind of derogatory manner. We've lived here for eleven years, and we've really gotten close to the folks in our neighborhood.

"I think the social success of children with disabilities hinges on whether they develop specific friendships. Jeanie has made two special friends. They fight like any kids do, but basically, the relationship has been wonderful. Jeanie does have some difficulty in social interaction. Sometimes she doesn't pick up on effective social cues like the way kids deal with her impulsive behavior or their discomfort when she is overtly affectionate. But these kids have been terrific at allowing those parts of her personality to exist without making her feel different.

"We have also noticed that Jeanie loves to play with smaller children. It creates a comfort zone for her. In many ways, she is behind developmentally. I have to work very hard to find a balance between letting her play at that childish level, because she is comfortable, and helping her to extend with her neighborhood friends, into standard relationships with children her own age. It is a very complicated structure, and it takes constant nurturing.

"The hardest thing for us is to define what is 'normal,' meaning what is socially acceptable normality, against what is normal for Jeanie Hartman. It's just like sorting out the protocol with Ritalin. For example, she's very comfortable playing with a four-year-old and a two-year-old, because she becomes the big friend, the big sister. But if I let her participate too long in this process, her behavior gets out of whack and she doesn't relate to her peer group effectively. That's when her friends in the neighborhood don't want to play with her.

"I'm constantly trying to keep the balance appropriate for Jeanie, between providing her with levels of comfort and yet edging her toward that painful normalcy that every parent with a child with a disability seeks out for the one they love. I don't want her to fall back into the trap of letting her peers take advantage of her, which used to result in them ridiculing and victimizing her."

"It is complicated, Cheri. I know in the world of children who are blind, families try to find the answers to their social glitch question all the time. And many blind adults never work it out. That's why they become comfortable only in the world of disability. Tell me about her brothers, Doug and Paul. How do they relate to their sister?"

"They're very different in their interactions with her. First of all, she has two brothers who are very different from each other. Doug takes on more of a parental role. He sees himself as a combination big brother and father figure. Now Paul gets caught in that middle child syndrome. What he said right from Jeanie's birth was that he was no longer the darling baby brother for Doug when she came along. Paul very much adores his older brother, and so he tends to be impatient with Jeanie. I know Paul loves his sister, but his older brother's affection is the most important thing to him. He feels that he's in a competitive circumstance, and probably believes he's in a lose-lose situation. If he spends a lot of time with Jeanie, he doesn't get to spend too much time with Doug. If he avoids Jeanie, or is impatient with her, Doug thinks he's a jerk. It's not easy to be a middle child, but it's particularly difficult in our family.

"Now let me give you a sense of how Doug functions; the other day I saw him teaching Jeanie the guitar. It was amazing, Tom. I'd never had the patience to do that with her, but Doug was great. He just stuck with it until she could play some chords. They have a wonderful closeness that I'm so grateful for. And I think they'll have it all of their lives."

"I understand that, Cheri. Because even though my sister, Peggy, was the sister who had to take care of me on a daily basis, my older sister, Jeanne, was the one I always tried to please. And I want to take this opportunity to say how sorry I am about the way I treated Peggy. Have you had to compensate by giving Paul more specific attention?"

"Yes, but that's true in any family. I just think parents have to become sensitive to the needs of each child on an individual basis. One of the benefits of having Jeanie in our family is that as I've learned to focus on her needs, I've also learned to pay attention to the needs of the two boys. That has been particularly helpful when dealing with Paul."

"I'm glad you discussed the boys, Cheri. I'm looking forward to meeting them. But tell me, is there a fuzziness in defining the difference between learning disability and Attention Deficit Disorder?"

"Yes, Tom, and it affects the way a child is integrated into the school system. Attention Deficit Disorder relates more to the behavior and socialization of a child than a learning disability (LD) does. A child can have both an LD problem, and ADD manifestations, so it's imperative for parents to be able to understand what issue their child is dealing with when they develop their IEP for the year. ADD has very important educational implications. The danger arises when a parent does not see any big problems with specific learning skills but notices difficulties with completing tasks or paying attention. This often leads a child to being considered a problem child or as having a behavior problem instead of being seen as a disabled student who needs special care and services. The LD child is much more likely to be identified. A student who is not LD, but is ADD, may be overlooked for referrals. This is most unfortunate. Schools need to be effectively informed by parents, who move the process forward."

My conversations with my friend Dr. David Hartman were different from those with Cheri, in that we conducted them at night. David is completely committed to his patients and his family, so his time is quite limited. Consequently, I was much more specific in our interview.

"David, I found in writing this book that all parents go through a period of denial. When I talked with Cheri, she mentioned that her professional skills may have enhanced her denial of Jeanie's Attention Deficit Disorder. Was that also true for you?"

"I think so, Tom. It was much easier for us to rationalize Jeanie's behavior and find more reasons to justify its occurring. But I don't think that's particularly unusual for parents who have a child with a disability. In our case, the old phrase 'A little knowledge can be dangerous' does apply. Let me expand on this. At two she was not picking up things quickly or adapting as early as other children. Cheri and I were able to point to somebody's study on delay, and then look at each other and say, 'Well, we don't have to worry, because the research data in this study indicates that children of our socio-economic background tend to behave this way.' To use Cheri's phrase, we were able to hide in the mumbo jumbo. In the end, we're no different from any other parents who go through denial, except that we can do a better job of finding a rationale for it."

"David, did your blindness contribute at all to a lack of awareness in picking up the cues?"

"I don't know, but probably the fact that Jeanie was physically small didn't strike me in the same way it did Cheri. I would hold this beautiful little girl and I got so used to her that I didn't project her against other children. To be fair, I probably did miss the physical differences, although I should also say, because I was so in love with this little child, I wasn't looking as hard."

"Were you disappointed when Jeanie had her first bout with illness?" I asked. "I mean, when your medical colleagues couldn't find the answers?"

"It was the first time I came up against the limitations of medicine in such a personal way. Maybe I need to correct that. I was never naive about what we can and can't do as physicians. But it had not been personal before. When I'd come home at night to see Jeanie so uncomfortable, or see Cheri under such stress, I was totally frustrated. The best analogy that I can give you is to think of my frustration over Jeanie like the frustrations you and I felt as little boys, when we wanted our peer group to accept us. We tried so hard to find avenues of connection. I was particularly alarmed when Jeanie had the body shutdowns after the chicken pox. We still don't have an explanation as to why they occurred. I also must admit that I think about the fact that the issue of potential lupus has not been completely resolved. When I consider my life as a physician, the problems we faced over Jeanie's health have served as a reality check for me."

"When did you first sense that Jeanie might have either a developmental delay or the potential for learning disability?"

"Not until Jeanie was in kindergarten. When our oldest son, Doug, was five, his teacher told us that he might have a learning problem. We chose not to do anything about it and it turned out that he's done fine. He has become a very capable student.

"When you deal with kids who are five, six, seven, and eight, there are wide variables of comprehension skills and attention spans. Consequently, if you jump on an issue too early, you can cause more problems than you do if you let it wait. We were not willing to make a hasty diagnosis about Jeanie that would send her down the wrong educational track.

"This approach of thinking everything through is very much a part of my personality. It's also an appropriate professional process. When I deal with patients who have complex psychiatric issues, I have to take my time and learn as much as I can about them before I move to diagnosis. And I admit, I agonize over decisions. I think Cheri and I are a good parental complement in that way. I don't mean that she just jumps in feet first, but she's more willing to become proactive early and go with her gut feelings."

"David, Cheri told me that when you decided to have Jeanie tested, even Dr. David Hartman, eminent psychiatrist, found the language used by the testers difficult to figure out. Is that right?"

"Tom, it was unbelievable," David said. "I work in the field of emotions every day, and I try to find appropriate words to convey emotional information to my patients. Here we were dealing with someone who was talking about the future of a child in such technical terms that I lost the true meaning of what she was attempting to get across to us. And I suppose this was when I came up against my own sense of personal denial."

"What do you mean?" I asked.

"This woman was giving us figures and ideas that only confused me. None of her words seemed to connect to the unique being I loved. I'm sure that other parents who come to these moments with their children feel like this, too. I want to be careful here, Tom, because I don't want to give the impression that I think testing is inappropriate. My goodness, we have to have a working sense of our children's problems, but in my business, I've learned that how people feel is much more important than statistical analysis."

"I agree with you," I said. "But I'm glad to hear you, as a parent and as a psychiatric professional, express it that way.

"David, I talked with Cheri about this earlier, but I'd be curious to see how you feel. There seems to be a large gray area when we discuss a child being learning disabled or having Attention Deficit Disorder. And I know that the child's educational track will depend on the way in which he or she is tested and perceived. Can you give parents some added guidelines when wrestling with the learning issues their child might be facing?"

"Learning disability is probably a continuum," David said. "I would guess that you and I, if carefully tested, would find that we have some areas where we do exceptionally well, and others where we do badly. For example, I'd always been a very good math student, but reading has never been a strength. I have always had a problem with language. Now, possibly, if I'd been carefully tested, somebody might have come up with the idea that I had an attention deficit, and then extended the diagnosis to suggest that I had a learning disability. Many of us deal with some form of learning disability. It's a lot like the difference between being totally blind and partially sighted. I've always had tremendous compassion for people who were partially deaf, partially blind, partially anything, because I feel that they struggle for a level of identity and an appropriate placement, both socially and educationally. The gray area in all of this is in trying to put appropriate labels on the issues so that solutions can be found. Cheri may have said this, but you understand there is a clear difference between learning disability and Attention Deficit Disorder, right?"

"I do, David, but go over Attention Deficit Disorder for me."

"There are three major factors that constitute Attention Deficit Disorder: At the level of activity, ADD kids are constantly presenting their teachers and their peers with a higher level of motor responses to stimulus. They can't slow down; their engines are always running.

"The second area is impulsiveness. ADD children do things without any forethought, and that makes the classroom situation difficult. When the ADD child is playing out all of his or her impulsive behaviors, it creates havoc for the other kids. They say, 'We wish we could do that, but we know it's socially inappropriate, so we'll just support the ADD child when he or she carries out that behavior.' Very often in classrooms, the child with Attention Deficit Disorder becomes the class clown, because that's the role that the other children want them to fill.

"The third area is that of focus. The child with Attention Deficit Disorder moves from activity to activity very rapidly. Frankly, it can drive people crazy, particularly in situations where a level of social order is required.

"Attention Deficit Disorder does not have to go hand in hand with learning disability, but it often does. So sorting out where your child fits in this equation is the number one issue for parents."

"David, how do you feel about the use of Ritalin?"

"I think that Ritalin protocols are wonderful. I've worked with children who are using Ritalin, and the results can be remarkable. As a society, we are so concerned with drug dependency that sometimes we miss how useful a drug protocol can be when correctly applied. That is certainly the case with Ritalin. The drug gives teachers an honest chance to evaluate a child. Children with Attention Deficit Disorder who slip through the cracks may be perceived as behavioral problems and can get so lost. If the interaction between the testers and psychiatry were better, so that Ritalin could be applied in more cases appropriately, I think kids would not get as labeled as they do.

"We just had a funny incident with Jeanie and Ritalin. We put her in ballet class. She had worked very hard to get ready for her recital. On recital day, she sat waiting to perform for so long that her Ritalin had worn off. Cheri and I sat in the audience, waiting for little Jeanie Hartman to bounce off the ceiling. We were sure that when she came to the critical part of the program, she would become socially inappropriate. So there we were holding hands, hoping she'd get through. And thank goodness she did, and she did just fine. We were able to breathe a huge sigh of relief. I don't think parents have to be afraid when they think about the use of this very helpful drug."

"David, how long are kids with ADD on Ritalin? Is there any research that indicates whether this continues into adulthood?"

"About seventy percent of the children who have Attention Deficit Disorder are plagued by these issues into adulthood. Of those, I don't know how many continue to use Ritalin, because as adults we find that what was considered a learning disability, or ADD, is evaluated as mental disorder, or psychiatric depression. I think this happens principally because the adult is no longer in school.

"And so the issues that relate to Attention Deficit Disorder become life questions, such as job placement, family structure, and all of the elements that go along with being a mature person. A number of these adults find their way to professionals like me, as alternatives to teachers and educational psychologists. I'm sure that if we studied them, we would find that many of these people suffering from mental illnesses whom I see in my practice may have been children with Attention Deficit Disorder.

"Essentially it comes down to this: Attention Deficit Disorder is a complex problem that tends to stay with a person throughout his or her life. It's hard to know how far Jeanie Hartman will go academically, but there is significant precedent. We've had Supreme Court justices with learning disabilities, and a number of very successful corporate executives who admit to having Attention Deficit Disorder, so I feel confident in Jeanie's future."

"You know, David," I said, "it seems to me this is probably a good place to end this conversation because, knowing you and Cheri, I also feel just as confident where Jeanie's concerned."

I received the following letter from Cheri upon her review of the Hartmans' chapter, which amplifies the unique commitment of these parents to their children, and the knowledge gained through years as competent professionals:

> I want to make a distinction that I think is important. I really do not believe that it is appropriate to diagnose a child as learning disabled when he or she is very young . . . not before kindergarten at any rate. It is too difficult to differentiate developmental delays within the normal range, and

delays that are precursors of learning disability. Observing a child's strengths and weaknesses is appropriate, and looking for a good match between the child and possible preschool options is smart.

In Jeanie's case, we did decide to have her stay an extra year in preschool. This is often appropriate for children who never show signs later of a persistent learning disability. There are children who do catch up with one extra year of school readiness activities. But it became evident to us during kindergarten that this catch-up process had not taken place adequately enough to put Jeanie on grade level. I feel that it is important not to mislead the reader into thinking that slight developmental delays should be interpreted as early signs of learning disabilities, or of Attention Deficit Disorder. Denial did come into play after Jeanie's diagnosis, but not a denial of her disability—it was more a denial of the impact that this disability might have on her life.

I have always held the belief that disabilities are context-defined. Blindness is not a disability in the right context. Being LD need not be disabling, given appropriate educational setting. I do strongly believe this, but it is denial to not admit that one is going to experience painful situations. We will not always be able to control the context that we have to experience. One of my earliest painful experiences was recognizing that The Achievement Center, about which I had such high expectations, would not be the solution I had hoped it would be; I was crushed to see in operation a methodology that I had learned was ineffective and truly detrimental.

I am now learning to face the reality that finding the right context for Jeanie's disability is going to be a constant challenge. This will take continual monitoring and re-evaluation.

I also want to clarify something that seemed confusing to me when I read our chapter. I'm not sure that it is clear to the reader that I believe that both Attention Deficit Disorder and Learning Disabilities are biological processes. One is probably not more biological than the other; they are distinguishable from each other, but not because one is more biological. They are distinctive diagnostically and in relation to treatments. Of course, saying that these processes are distinguishable does not mean that they are not related; they definitely can contribute to each other, but it is advantageous to understand them as separate processes.

One point that I especially want to stress is that the student who is not learning disabled, but has an Attention Deficit, may be overlooked for referrals, and this is most unfortunate. This is the child likely to be considered a "bad kid," or a behavioral problem, instead of being identified and in need of positive attention and appropriate help. My work with the teenagers in the high school has really enforced this belief.

C H A P T E R

Jim and Anita

HAL O'LEARY IS THE PERSON whom I respect most in the field of disability. Hal and his staff have taught over 50,000 people with disabilities to ski in Winter Park, Colorado, in a program called the National Sports Center for the Disabled. Patty and I, along with our children, Blythe and Tom, have been skiing there for fifteen years and plan to build a home that allows us to be closer to this mountain full of miracles on a regular basis. I once asked Hal to tell me which group of people with disabilities he felt closest to. He didn't even hesitate.

"Children with Down syndrome," he said. "I believe they are God's most wonderful creations."

"Why?" I asked.

"Even though their physical disability is obvious, every child with Down syndrome I have ever known seems to possess a uniqueness of spirit."

My friend's comments were completely validated when I had a chance to meet Kevin Wagner and his family. Jim and Anita Wagner, their daughter, Jamie, and their son, Kevin, live in Denver, Colorado. Jim runs an independent remodeling and construction company. Jamie is a sixteen-year-old, totally involved in school, swimming, and boys—not necessarily in that order. Kevin is a thirteen-year-old young man with Down syndrome, celebrating life with every ounce of his being. Anita is one of the most dynamic women I have ever met—fighting the good fight for her family on the front lines of the disability battlefield and changing everybody's perception about what's possible for a child with Down syndrome. Our interview took place on a Sunday afternoon in the Wagner home. Although we talked for seven hours, I never even realized what time it was. These people were so incredible and their story so intriguing, I was completely captivated by their courage, their joy, and the drama of their lives. After learning that Jim and Anita had met while attending the University of Colorado and had fallen in love on Anita's twenty-first birthday, I started off with the question I have asked every family: "Anita, were the pregnancies of Jamie and Kevin normal?"

"Completely, Tom," she said. "Jamie was a perfect little girl and the pregnancy was easy. Nothing out of the ordinary happened during the time I was carrying Kevin until the last week. Then the roof fell in."

"What do you mean?" I asked.

"A week before I went into labor and Kevin was born, I got a call about seven in the morning from my father. He was panicked. He said, 'They have taken your mom to the hospital, and she is dead.'

"I said, 'No, that can't be.'

"And he said, 'It's true, dear, she's dead.'

"I rushed to the hospital, and there was no denying it.

"It's amazing what we do as human beings. The day after

the funeral I started to have contractions while I was at my father's house. I was writing thank-you notes to people who had expressed their sadness about my mother's death. I was committed to getting them all done before I had this baby. I was very organized, very focused. That was how I survived.

"My father and I decided to walk around the block in order to ease the labor pains, and I realized I needed to get home. When I got back to the house with my father, there was just enough time for Jim and I to get to the hospital, and then Kevin was born."

"Jim, where were you when all this was going on?" I asked.

"I was at our house taking care of Jamie. It was such a confusing week. Anita wanted to be with her father, but somebody had to watch Jamie. We really were splintered."

"Before we talk about Kevin's birth, can you define Down syndrome?"

Jim said, "Whereas most people have forty-six chromosomes, Kevin has forty-seven. He has an extra, twenty-first chromosome."

"Jim, do we know why this happened?" I asked.

"No we don't. It is a genetic fluke—it just happens. There is one rare type of Down syndrome that one can inherit, but that's not typical. Trisomy twenty-one is a fluke. There is no genetic crossover; Jamie's chances for having a child with Down syndrome are only minimal."

"Then nothing during the pregnancy indicated that there might have been something wrong?"

"That's right, Tom," Anita said. "I had no indications that we had anything to worry about."

"So neither of you have a sense of guilt about this, do you?"

"No," Jim said. "This problem occurs right at conception, during the initial cell division, and it is totally random."

"So basically the labor was as normal as it could be, and Kevin was born. When was the first time you realized that there might be something different?"

Anita said, "The first moment I knew anything was wrong was when they handed Kevin to me and I looked at his little hands. I should tell you that I have very short, stubby hands from my mother's side of my family. And Jamie has long beautiful hands. I remember when she was born, I was so impressed with her hands. But when I looked at Kevin's hands, I knew something was wrong. There was no time to think, because they abruptly took him away."

"Were you there, Jim?" I asked.

"I was right next to her. But I think I was a little rocky from everything that had been going on, so I didn't pick up on this as instantly as Nita did."

"Jim, were you surprised that they took Kevin away so quickly?"

"A little bit, but not totally. He was sort of bluish and they said they had to warm him. That seemed to make sense. There wasn't a reason for me to panic."

"I guess it really breaks down to mother's instinct," I said.

"That's right," they agreed.

Anita said, "I just noticed the hands and nobody responded. Out in the hall was the pediatrician. He was a very young doctor, and he was terrified to tell me about Kevin. Thank God I had a great gynecologist, Dr. Gottesfield, who has become a really important friend. He said to the pediatrician, 'You get in there and tell her what's going on, because she knows something's happening.' I guess they almost duked it out just outside my room. There was a hell of a lot of friction between the two of them.

"They finally came in, and the pediatrician said to me, 'Anita, we think your baby has Down syndrome.' I freaked."

"You weren't alone," Jim said. "So did I. And this guy had no sensitivity at all. He was one of those doctors who had been trained to always offer a level of positive medical possibility, but he had absolutely no human skills. He alienated both of us."

Anita said, "I was never so devastated. We had just buried my mother a couple of days before and now this young doctor was telling me that my baby had Down syndrome. How were we supposed to cope with this? Thank God we had friends. They came to visit us right away. I have a special friend, Helen, who also had a baby at about the same time that Kevin was born. When she came to visit me, I was holding Kevin. She picked him up, looked at him and said, 'He is an absolutely beautiful baby.' The nurses loved him. Children who have Down syndrome are wonderful babies. That's a blessing for mothers and fathers because other people warm to them easily. That happened with Kevin in the first few days of life.

"I know that most of the parents you are interviewing found out their children had disabilities later on."

"That's right," I said. "In the case of deaf, blind, or CP children, the issue doesn't manifest itself for a number of months."

"We had to face Kevin's Down syndrome right away," Anita said. "There was no time for denial, no time to bond with the child, no time to find out about all the special things that Kevin was before being hit with this devastating news. Oh, God, I'm not proud of this, but I have to admit I didn't want him. In those first few days there were times when I wished he would go to sleep at night and just not wake up."

Jim took her hand.

"I can't believe you're telling me that, Anita," I said. "I know how much you love Kevin now. It's hard for me to comprehend that you ever felt that way."

"She did," Jim told me, "because she didn't have time to

bond. Also she was reacting to the overall losses in her life. She was very close to her mother, so that death, coupled with Kevin's birth was just too much for her."

"I can understand that," I said. "Were you feeling the same way, Jim?" I asked.

"I was working very hard to find the ability to cope with the problem. I remember coming into Nita's hospital room and saying, 'Look, Nita, we have this beautiful baby boy and he has a problem, but that problem is only part of who he is. I believe he can grow and be many other things.'"

"Boy, I'm glad you told me that, Jim," I said, "because that's what I believe. If someone were to ask me what I want them to understand when they think of Tom Sullivan, blind person, it's easy for me to tell them. I want them to believe that blindness is only one part of who I am, not the whole person. It's so fortunate that you two have the kind of relationship that allowed you to operate from different perspectives and yet find a common ground to build on."

"Jim is a rock," Anita said. "He has the capacity to search until he finds the appropriate way to solve a problem. I am extremely creative, but I might come up with ten different ways to come to approach an issue. Jim might think of the same ten, but he'll continue searching and sorting out until he selects one solid path to the answer and stays on it."

"You know, folks," I said, "throughout the writing of this book, within the family units that work, this is how parents seem to cope: two different personalities bringing their best to a common ground that allows them to find solutions and allows their children to grow."

Anita said, "When I was in the hospital, my pediatrician wanted me to leave the next day. Thank goodness I had Dr. Gottesfield. He came into my room, sat down on my bed, and said, 'Anita, you stay here as long as you want. I have a child with cerebral palsy. When he was born, I didn't know how we would survive, but that was largely because I didn't know who this wonderful person was. Given time, I came to understand that he was a whole person who happened to have a disability.'

"I'm so grateful for that doctor, Tom. He let me stay in the hospital and he gave me those words of encouragement. It gave me something to begin to build on.

"I will also be grateful to a little boy named Teddy who had Down syndrome, and to his mother, Nora. They came to visit me on the third day I was in the hospital. Teddy climbed up on the bed. He had excellent language skills, so we had a conversation. He was a beautiful boy. I started to think, 'Maybe Kevin can be like Teddy; maybe I can get through this.'"

Jim said, "I observed Nita watching this little boy, and I could actually see the change in her eyes. I guess people don't know the impact they can have on others, but that afternoon I saw a beginning. When you have the kind of positive family strength we have, a beginning is all you need to build on."

"So you brought Kevin home," I said. "You've had a chance to meet Teddy and his mother, but you've got Jamie to take care of. And now you've got a brand new baby who has Down syndrome. Was there a lot of stress for both of you?"

"There really was," Jim said. "Although our friends were very supportive, it was difficult for my parents. They were uncomfortable with the situation and could only talk about Kevin in terms of his 'illness.' Some people are better equipped to cope with something like this than others; it's just part of their personality. The strain of trying to build my new business and keep things on track for Jamie, along with supporting Nita with Kevin, was almost overwhelming. When I look back at all of it now, it seems like a blur. Actually until you brought all this up today, I hadn't thought about it very much. But as we sit here, I find it amazing that we got through the beginning stages."

Anita said, "Prior to Kevin's birth, I had an intensely close extended family. I talked to my grandmother and my mother every day. I couldn't sneeze without my aunts, my uncles, my mom, and my grandmother knowing. And then it was gone. My mother, you see, was the matriarch. She held us all together, so when she died my extended family had a very difficult transition period. We really felt like two people, Jim and I, who lived on an island, and we had to completely believe in each other and make our own family the foundation for a new life. I'm astounded that it worked out."

"You talked earlier of your friends. Pick out one or two examples of how terrific they were in those early stages."

Jim said, "We have to start with Jimmy and Gay Sanwick. They are Kevin's godparents, and I can't even begin to measure the impact they have had on our lives. The Sanwicks live in Tulsa, Oklahoma, but I had grown up with them. I skied with Jimmy all through my childhood—at your beloved Winter Park—so we had stayed close over the years.

"When Kevin was about six weeks old, Jimmy called and said that we just had to bring Kevin to Tulsa to visit them. We looked at each other and thought, 'How could we possibly go to Oklahoma now, with this six-week-old baby and all of the issues that we were coping with?' But Jimmy kept talking, and he finally convinced us to show up. We packed up the car and drove to Tulsa."

Anita interrupted. "I can remember walking into the house. We started talking right away. Jimmy looked at us and said, 'He's adorable. He's simply adorable. I was so afraid. I didn't know what he was going to look like, but Nita and Jim, he is adorable.' Now, I'm not particularly a religious person, Tom, but his next line so touched me, I'll never forget it. He said, 'You know, Nita, God doesn't make junk.' It stopped us dead in our tracks."

"I understand," I said. "What a concept Jimmy came up with. 'God doesn't make junk.' I believe that."

Anita went on. "Gay looked at Jim and me and said, 'I know there are still memories to be made and we are going to start making them on this trip.' Do you believe that, Tom?"

"It is one of the greatest lines I have ever heard," I said.

"We really bought into that," Jim told me. "It was our first step toward adjustment. We began to think that there was hope, that we could find a way to make this work, and that Kevin's life would have value. We had come to a turning point. We had made a decision that we needed to remain a family. Even though we had Kevin and even though lots of things were going to be different now, we couldn't live his life. He needed to fit in the life of our family."

Jim continued. "We've always had such a good marriage and through the darkest days we've always communicated. My view at the time was, this may not have been the baby we dreamed of, but he was ours. Anita was hoping for Mary Poppins to arrive, but when she didn't show up at our house, Anita took on the responsibility of being the best mother she could be. She learned everything there was to know about Down syndrome to give Kevin the best possible life, and I think it's worked out that way."

Anita said, "We were turning the corner. In those first few weeks, my sense of Down syndrome was completely distorted. Before anybody knew much about children with Down syndrome, these beautiful youngsters were called Mongoloids. People often imagined them as little monsters with small heads, big shoulders, and lolling tongues. Mongoloid children were always institutionalized. Even though I had been a teacher, that's sort of what I believed. It's not easy to believe that your child will have a good life when you've been conditioned to think that would be impossible for children with this disability."

"Something you said before, Jim, is worth repeating," I said. "You had a great marriage and good communication, and even in those early days you kept working together."

"That's right, Tom. We never stopped communicating. After a while, time made sure that knowledge and experience caught up. And we also got to know, love, and enjoy Kevin."

I could sense Anita's agitation.

"I didn't get to that place about Kevin overnight. It's true that Jimmy and Gay's encouragement, along with Teddy, were really important. We were beginning to build foundations for our family's future, but we weren't there yet. When we first brought Kevin home, he would go to bed at night and I would wish that he wouldn't wake up the next morning."

"Anita, I have to ask you this. There are many parents all over this country who feel just like you both did. They will read this book. I want you to know that I'm going to write your words just the way you said them. Is that all right?"

"Yes it is. I think it is important. I feel appalled now and saddened about how I felt toward my baby, but those feelings were very real. I couldn't hate this little boy when I was holding him, only when I wasn't. So I would get up in the middle of the night in order to overcome these negative feelings and I would sit and rock him because when I was holding him I couldn't hate him. When he wasn't there, I could remember what our life used to be like, and I would say to myself, 'What will our lives be now?'"

"Anita, I have to help here," I broke in. "I don't think it was a question of hating this little baby. Rather, you did not want to have to go through the pain. You were saying, 'I didn't want this life.'"

Jim said, "We've talked about it many times this way. It's not so much that she didn't want the child, she just didn't want the life."

"Jim, did you feel out of control during this period?" I asked.

"I'm one of those guys who builds and fixes things. But now I thought, 'I can't fix this.' This is simply the way it was. I felt totally out of control. Here was a situation that I could not change. I hated watching Nita go through this kind of pain. And even though we kept communicating and I knew we loved each other, I felt as if I was waiting in limbo for something to happen. I don't know how parents get through a time like this."

"But you proved they do," I said.

"Somehow they do," they agreed.

Anita said, "A sense of humor is so important in all of this. I remember telling Jim that we would keep Kevin if he didn't have any other disabilities. But for the first three weeks of his life, I wasn't sure he could hear. So I would walk up behind him and clap my hands to see if he would startle. I was so sure he was deaf. And I remember saying to Jim, 'Maybe I could cope with a child that's deaf. And maybe I could cope with just the Down syndrome. But both is too much.'"

"Tom, you asked us to talk about other friends that impacted us," Jim said, "and I remember the story about Anita's friend Dana."

"That's right," Anita said. "Dana came to the door when Kevin was about four weeks old with a baby gift and said, 'I know all about your mom, and I know your baby has Down syndrome, but I just had to come by.'

"'Well, he's over there in the cradle,' I replied, 'so you can look at him yourself.'

"She walked over to Kevin, picked him up, and yelled at me, 'Anita, you dumb shit. He's a beautiful baby. I don't want to hear any negatives. Look at this child. Take a look at this child. He's wonderful.'

"That jolted me. My friend felt comfortable with Kevin. Now I know it's easy for people to say they can handle it when they're not with a disability twenty-four hours a day, but it is amazing what perspective you can get from outside people who love you."

"I suppose," I said, "that you get to the point where reality hits and you have to decide what to do about Kevin's future."

They both laughed.

"Kevin's future," Jim said. "When you live with Nita, you don't think about the future because she's too busy in the present. From day one of Kevin's life, Anita was doing something. When she was still in the hospital, she sent me to the library to find all the literature on Down syndrome, and that wasn't enough. She made me get stuff on every kind of disability she could think of. She was reading right from the beginning."

Anita laughed. "Kevin was in a program when he was a week old. People started coming to the house right from the beginning. On the one hand, I was devastated, but on the other I was an overachiever. I thought, 'Damn it, I've got to do it, I've got to know what to do, I've got to know everything there is to know about Down syndrome, because if I miss a minute we may not do everything right.'"

Jim said, "When I think of that period, what strikes me most vividly is our friends; they always got behind us and got so involved. They came out of the woodwork and formed a support network behind us because of everything our family had been through. And it has remained that way. Our friends have continued to participate in our lives with the most wonderful feeling of love and human interaction anyone could ever experience."

Anita added, "They allowed me the time I needed to search for answers that I sure didn't find in the literature."

She laughed.

"I mean, what they said about kids with Down syndrome, even thirteen years ago, was amazing. All the literature had been written about children who had been institutionalized. Even before we went to Tulsa, I can remember reading an article that said your child won't ever be able to eat by himself and he's not going to be able to go to the bathroom alone. Then there was a ridiculous article published in some medical journal that I find funny now. It said that children with Down syndrome have skin that doesn't tan. Well, of course, it didn't tan. They were always in institutions."

We all started to laugh, but Anita's next comment shut the laughter off quickly.

She said, "The literature gave me the impression that Kevin would be a helpless, drooling monster."

"So where do you get the hope?" I asked.

"I suppose it comes from networking with other parents. We're all reaching for the same goal."

Jim said, "And if enough of us believe it's possible, we can at least make it probable."

"So let me see if I can set the scene. You got Kevin involved with an occupational therapist and a physical therapist from day one. But you had to plan a potential track for him, both mentally and physically. Did you have anyone to talk to?"

Anita said, "I went to The Kennedy Center here in Denver. At that time, it was a referral center for parents of children with disabilities. While I was there, I met a doctor. My conversation with him changed my point of view. He asked me if I felt sorry for Kevin, and I told him that I couldn't begin to feel sorry for Kevin until I had finished feeling sorry for myself. The doctor looked at me and said, 'That's very interesting, Mrs. Wagner, because most people don't admit that. They are always transferring their feelings of sorrow to their children.'

"I said, 'I want somebody to tell me when this will stop hurting.'

"He looked at me again and said, 'It will never stop hurting,

Anita. The pain will change, but there will always be times when you hurt.'

"That was very helpful. I no longer had to wait for the magic day when the pain would disappear. That made it more manageable. I knew that I was striving for a goal that I wouldn't achieve in two weeks. For me, it changed from a problem to a process. I knew the hurt would lessen, the intensity would change, and that I would have to cope with moments throughout our whole lives that would always be painful."

"Has that remained the case?" I asked.

"Yes," Anita said. "What I didn't know then but I understand now is that there would be many more highlights than pain. And if I were to put a percentage on it, I believe that at least ninety percent of Kevin's life has been joyous. That's not bad for anybody."

"Babies are babies," Jim said, "and as long as they are loved, they're okay. The parents deal with the early problems—the emotional ones. Anita used to come home from a shopping trip with Kevin and say, 'Sometimes I feel so alone. I walk through the shopping mall and I have this little baby with Down syndrome. Even though I know I exaggerate, I feel like there is a light on his head that keeps saying, Down syndrome, Down syndrome, and everybody's watching."

Anita interrupted. "I feel as if we're on an island. I knew we had wonderful friends, but before Kevin was his own person, we had to deal with the tremendous sense of isolation like all parents of children with disabilities."

Jim said, "We might be giving you a mixed message, but maybe that's the way life is. We did the best we could. I still had a business to run. Most of the burden, in this early period, was on Nita's shoulders. But I can't say it strongly enough—many fathers hurt, too. They feel a different kind of pain because generally they're not involved in the daily care. They live with their own level of complete frustration."

"Did you ever feel that way?" I asked.

"No, I was one of the lucky ones. It never dawned on me that my life wouldn't be fulfilled by Nita, Kevin, and Jamie. But I am sensitive to the struggle of many fathers."

"You're right, Jim. We tend to think of the fathers who can't cope as nothing but losers or cowards, or worse. I suppose behind every person there is a story."

We all agreed.

"Jim, please describe the different ways you two participate as Kevin's parents."

"Well, Nita is all about fire and passion. But she is also about intelligence and commitment and child rights."

"Thank you, dear," Anita said. "And if we're doling out compliments, I know I said before that you were a great problem-solver and that you were incredibly steady, but I don't think we should give the impression that you're also not passionate about Kevin's issues. You just take a pragmatic approach, and I think we balance each other in just the right way. When we talk about the parent relationship, one of the dangers is that others might get the impression that the moms are doing most of the work both in the home and as advocates. But in our case, Jim is just as likely to bake cookies with the kids as I am to go out in the front yard and throw a baseball with them. We have always had a level of real sharing that makes it all work."

"I suppose what we're talking about is shadings. Is that right?" I asked.

"Yes," Jim said. "It is a question of shadings, and playing the game to your strengths. That's what we do."

"Other than the way you work on Kevin's behalf, are there other elements in the parenting process and the overall family dynamic that we ought to be talking about?"

"I think so," Anita said. "Being involved on Kevin's behalf is one of my passions, but it's not my only one. I don't want the disability to define our family any more than I want it to define

Kevin. It is a piece of us, but there are so many other parts to our family outside of Kevin's disability. And even though working on behalf of families who have children with disabilities has become my focus, I don't want it to become the sole, dominant part of my life. We have friends who have kids with disabilities, but frankly more of our friends have typical kids. There has to be balance."

Jim said, "We just don't want our family to be seen as a 'disabled family,' but a family where disability is just one of the issues we deal with every day."

"Tom, here is the best example I can give you," Anita said. "I was in the middle of a master's program in child development when Kevin was born. I actually finished the degree. I met a woman who had a child with Down syndrome. She told me that I needed to find a way to get on with my life, and that along with meeting Kevin's needs, I needed to have a sense of purpose for myself. I went back to school and got my master's degree when Kevin was eight months old."

"Something else came out of those early conversations," Jim said. "Another parent said to us, 'Kevin can be the scapegoat for everything you don't do in your lives, but it's not going to be the baby, it's going to be *you* who suffers. He can ruin your marriage and Jamie's life. You may never travel, and Anita probably won't finish her master's, but this little baby cannot be responsible for all the things you don't do. You simply can't blame your failures on him.' That felt like someone slapping us across the face and saying, 'Get it together, people.' As a result, we've gone out of our way to focus on our family dynamic and our individual abilities. We have not allowed the disability to overwhelm us."

Anita said, "I remember when Joyce, a wonderful woman, took me to see some closed workshops for the disabled. That's where you see the most difficult problems associated with the

Down community. She said, 'Look, if you know the worst, then you can cope with that and work toward the best that Kevin can be.' That was a reality check. It made me frame all the potentials of Kevin's life—good and bad—and that was healthy."

"I understand now that you've made these fundamental decisions, Anita, but you had to get Kevin on a track. So where did he begin?"

"We placed him in an infant stimulation program," Anita said, "and here I was trying to be supermom. By then I had decided that Kevin was our baby, and that we were going to do everything possible to enhance his life. So if they told us to roll him on the ball to stimulate his muscles for five minutes, I rolled him on the ball for thirty minutes. If they said, 'Help him move his arms and legs in patterns of exercise for ten minutes,' I did it for an hour. If they said, 'Expose him to visual stimulus,' I made sure that he was so overstimulated that he probably thought I was weird even at those early stages. I absolutely overcompensated.

"I was segmenting all of these areas of Kevin's life rather than dealing with him holistically. This was a little boy named Kevin, and his first and foremost need was to develop a complete personality. Boy, I did everything wrong. The most dangerous parent is the one who has a degree in early childhood development! I tried to find an academic approach that framed the way I dealt with our child until Kevin was about eighteen months old. Then, suddenly, the light bulb came on. I don't know why—I can't point to a specific moment—but somehow my brain clicked on the idea that it was more important for Kevin to be doing the same things that other kids did and that I should be putting Jim's and my creative skills to work facilitating normalcy rather than expanding disability."

"So what did you do?" I asked.

"We became rebels," Jim said. "Actually, Jamie made us go through this turning point in our approach. She needed the kind of attention from us that any three-year-old does. We felt we had two choices: either to separate, with one of us taking Kevin and working on his disability, while the other spent time with Jamie, or to act like a family. We fundamentally believe in the philosophy of family participation. So we actually did double duty for a while. We tried to provide Kevin with all the special activities, but we also spent a lot of time just doing things together as a family. And we learned that we could facilitate Kevin's needs much more appropriately by exposing him to family and community than by isolating him in segmented activities."

Jim went on. "The battle we felt inside about what Kevin should or shouldn't have was about programs versus instinct. We were not experts and we felt that we needed to go to experts to get the appropriate help we believed Kevin should have. I don't want to indicate that the system can't provide children with important tools, but the system has to be applied based on parental instinct. This may sound strange, but I think every parent of a child with a disability can find these correct instincts somewhere inside."

"I believe that, too," I said. "I think back to my mother, when I was born blind and there was no help for her. Yet she chose to raise me in conjunction with community."

"That's the decision we made," Anita said.

I laughed. "And now that I've had the chance to meet Kevin, I understand why that was such a great decision. He's an incredibly well-adjusted child."

"He is," Anita said, "but there's still a long road. Anyway, we trusted our instinct, and I know we're better off for it. I would go to places where kids with Down syndrome were being segregated and I'd simply come home sad. I tried a number of programs, but the best thing that ever happened to Kevin was when he started to play with kids in the community."

"Anita, I think you're a little ahead of yourself," Jim said. "Remember, we went back and forth, in and out of the system, until Kevin was about two and a half. We were sitting one night at dinner and you said, 'Jim, do you think we've had Kevin for fifty years? I'm exhausted.' I agreed with you. The constant effort that parents have to put forward to find the right system for their child is exhausting."

Anita interrupted with excitement. "Earlier you were asking us if there was a turning point, and there really was, when Kevin was about two and a half. He was in the third program we had tried in Denver. The administrators decided that they were going to bus all these kids with disabilities every day. And I started to think about that. I couldn't imagine any other two-and-a-half-year-old getting on a bus to go somewhere. So I decided to get on the bus with him to check it out.

"At seven in the morning the bus ride from hell began. We drove all over the city to pick up every one of these babies with a variety of disabilities, and I became more and more upset. When we got to Cheeseman Park—that's a park in central Denver—four buses came together. They were all loaded with a mixed bag of kids. But when they took our kids off one bus and put them on what was decided were the appropriate buses to take them to the right infant stimulation program, I lost it. I thought, 'These are two-and-a-half-year-old babies and we're schlepping them around the entire city of Denver.'"

"So what did you do?" I asked.

"I got off the bus in tears and walked over to the social worker assigned to these kids and said, 'This is just not going to work. Kevin can't even look out the window. Essentially what you people are asking me to do is put my baby on a bus for an hour and a half to get here to spend two hours being stimulated, and then put him back on the bus for an hour and a half to get home when he can't even look out a window. He's being locked up to sit for three hours, totally unstimulated, looking at the back of a bus seat, and you call this good for my child?'

"That was the day I became a Parent Advocate. I started to talk to other parents, saying, 'Excuse me . . . excuse me. If you haven't ridden the bus with your child, you ought to do it.' So then we as parents decided to change the system for babies on the bus. Until we got them seats from which they could at least see out of a window, nobody was going to ride the bus. We got together a coalition of about twelve parents of children with different disabilities, and we made the administrators change the system."

"Boy, I'm delighted to hear that, Anita, because that's the focus of this book. I want all parents of children with disabilities to read it and say to themselves, *'We need to coalesce. We need to understand we're part of a common community. We need to understand that our common ground and our common purpose is the education, growth, and emotional welfare of our children.'*"

Jim raised his glass in a toast. "To Tom Sullivan and all of the parent crusaders."

We clinked glasses and felt bonded.

Anita said, "Parents who have kids with disabilities need to begin working right from the start to help their children become part of the community. We were so lucky on this block. There were two families with little boys the same age as Kevin. Whenever Kevin would do something that I considered a little weird, I'd think, 'I don't know if this is Down syndrome or whether it's just about being a little boy.' So I'd call my friend Helen and I'd say, 'Has Justin ever done this?' Most of the time, Helen would say, 'Yeah.' We would find that there was much more common ground between our children than areas that were dissimilar. So right from infancy, Kevin was able to interact with Justin and his other friend, Brad."

"Kevin was very lucky," I said. "I didn't have that situation, and I know how alone I was."

Jim said, "I think you make your own luck, Tom. I don't mean that you could as a little boy, but I think that people who are always searching for the right answers will know them when they come along, and be able to make their own luck."

"I think Kevin's success track came from community," Anita said. "When he was two and a half, and I was trying to decide on a preschool, Kevin's little friends, Justin and Brad, made me understand that they wanted him to go to school with them. I thought, 'Why the hell not?' So, I went to Jamie's preschool—where all the kids in our community go—and I said to the teacher, 'We can't figure out why Kevin can't go to school here.'

"And she said, 'I don't know why not.'

"But the director expressed, 'I'm not sure that we can address Kevin's special needs.'

"So I replied, 'Kevin needs to be part of this community because he was born here. He needs to hear typical kids' language and have the same experiences they have. We will provide all the extra help: the physical, speech, and occupational therapy. You just have to let him be here.' And they did! The only alteration to the program was to put Kevin into a three-year-old classroom when he was four. Up to that point, he had been on much the same track as the other children, with one exception. Kevin had learned sign language to communicate.

"Many babies who have Down syndrome don't develop oral language skills since the muscles around their mouths are so weak. Instead, they learn sign language. Happily, all of the kids in Kevin's preschool began to learn sign language too—and loved it."

Jim said, "One of the social workers that Anita talked to at that point told her that she was afraid if a child with Down syndrome learned sign language, he would look like a monkey.

Anita got pretty upset, and said, 'I don't care if he looks like a two-headed person. He needs to communicate.'"

"Back to parent instinct again," I said. "Since I've been writing this book, I've been hearing the word *inclusion*, and you just made me understand how it works in the best way. It's not just setting up a classroom that can be thought of as an artificial laboratory where kids are thrown together and the results are measured. The community is an important part of the equation. Inclusion is what we're all reaching for, but when it's not working for everyone involved, it's 'dumping.'"

"You've got it, Tom," Anita said. "Over the years, I've seen so many children with disabilities who, in the name of 'inclusion,' have been dumped into classrooms without appropriate support. Good inclusion must have appropriate supports."

"It seems that, unlike other disabilities, it is hard to categorize what people with Down syndrome can and can't achieve."

"You are right," Jim said. "You're getting into an area that we're sensitive about: the question of testing and categorization."

"Today I sat here with Kevin," I said, "and every once in a while he would say something that knocked me right back on my heels. The boy sitting opposite me would have a light bulb come on. I felt as if I were hit with a laser because he was so direct and accurate in assessing personality."

"Let's talk about that in an educational context," Anita said, "because it relates very much to the way kids get handled in school. They used to tell us that even if Kevin were pretty much on a par with his peers, at some point, he would plateau. So I waited for the moment when Kevin would put on the brakes. But as an educator, I recognized that he never really plateaued. Now I've seen certain parts of his educational process slow down. For example, when he is learning to read, he may not be as physically active. But he has never found that stopping place they call 'plateau.' Certainly there are gaps between Kevin and his peers, but they're not insurmountable. He's always working on something and progressing.

"All schools require a child developing his first IEP to take a standard battery of tests. The last time Kevin took the I.Q. test, he was about six years old. The test couldn't tell us anything that the team of people working with him for several years didn't already know."

"Parents really have to know their children," Jim said, "and we're all so grateful that Anita held the line on this point."

"I.Q. is an excellent test to determine language comprehension," Anita continued, "but I do not believe it gives us an accurate estimate of a person's intelligence."

"But you must have faced a lot of pain," I said, "when you came to the question of Kevin's education. This is where parents and systems usually collide."

"They do, Tom," Jim said. "We needed to be extremely assertive to be sure everyone was focused on Kevin's needs, not just on what the district wanted for him."

Anita noted, "We took an aggressive approach toward Kevin's education. I knew from my own teaching experience that we had to work together to develop a creative IEP for Kevin. This is not often the case; many times teams just go through the motions. In Kevin's case, the team emphasized the least-restrictive environment, and he spent as much time as possible his kindergarten year in a classroom with typical kids.

"Kevin was 'mainstreamed.' He went to school with children who had no major disabilities. But he did not experience true inclusion. An aide stood by Kevin's table to tell him how to do the work. Finally, after he had been in regular kindergarten for a couple of months, Kevin went up to the teacher and said, 'I want to sit at one of the smart tables.'"

Jim said, "The teacher had broken the classroom up into

three groups and Kevin felt the separation. He wanted to be at the smart table, so when one of the 'smart' kids was absent, Kevin would just go ahead and sit in his seat. He found his own solution to the problem."

"Jim and Anita, that's fantastic," I said. "I wish I'd had those kinds of guts when I was a kid."

"I wish you had had a kindergarten teacher like Kevin's," Jim replied. "A great teacher teaches the whole child. Michelle Roth was a wonderful advocate for him that year. She came full circle and really supported us when we needed to get involved in his first-grade IEP."

"I started looking for appropriate alternatives for Kevin in January of his kindergarten year," Anita said. "Now the system was saying to me, 'There are no options. All kids with Down syndrome go into SLICC—Severely Limited Intellectual Capacity Classes.' I said, 'That's not what the law says.' I asked them, 'Have you heard about the least-restricted environment clause? The law says that a child must be given inclusion to the maximum extent possible, and here in Denver children are being slotted according to category, not evaluated according to need.'

"So I started to evaluate what was available and I have never been so depressed. It was just devastating. These classrooms all reminded me of handicap jail. They were always in the basement or at the far end of the hall. The teachers had lost the joy of teaching. All they really were doing was monitoring behavior and yelling at kids to shut up. There was no way Kevin would waste his time in one of those classrooms. I felt as if I were putting a butterfly in a mason jar, closing the lid, and watching this beautiful creature slowly die. I believed that if we allowed Kevin into one of those classrooms, he would simply suffocate. So then I started looking at traditional classrooms."

"You mean classrooms that did not have kids with disabilities in them?" I asked.

"That's right," Anita said. "I knew that I was in for a battle, but that seemed to be the only reasonable alternative. I called Michelle Roth, Kevin's kindergarten teacher, and explained, 'We really have to come together when we have Kevin's first-grade IEP and bring a lot of creative interest to that meeting.'

"I believe that sometimes fate intervenes. At that time, I was teaching at Jamie's school. One of the teachers there kept saying, 'Why can't we have Kevin here? He's a child, and we're in the children business.'

"And I said, 'I don't think you understand. Kevin doesn't have the focused concentration that these kids do.' My concern was that if Kevin was not in a traditional public school and a special classroom, he would fall between the cracks.

"But this wonderful teacher, Anne Breckinridge, kept telling me, 'Anita, a child is a child.' And she talked me into letting Kevin come to visit her classroom at the Stanley British Primary School. Because Kevin felt so comfortable, and because the school had taken such an inclusive approach toward having him, it became apparent to me that there was no other place for my son. And so, at his IEP meeting, I was not going to take no for an answer. What we found was that British Primary met Kevin's social and emotional needs. Kevin remained in this positive school setting for the next six years. I believe the boy you sat with today and found so engaging owes much of who he is to that most positive educational environment."

"But, Anita, what happened with Kevin's IEP?"

"Well, even though Kevin was at British Primary, we'd written his IEP so that he could be on dual enrollment with Denver public schools. That way he could get the special-education services he needed. Actually, it was to guarantee that he receive all he was entitled to under state and federal law."

"I know from talking to Kevin earlier that he can read, write, and do simple math. That's unusual for children with Down syndrome. Is Kevin where he is today because you constantly tweaked the system and found the appropriate loopholes?"

"Any system is imperfect," Jim said, "but as parents, we must understand our rights and work to find a common ground with educational professionals. These professionals are on the side of the parent. They're overworked, underpaid people, but generally they are on the side of the parents. Parents *can* get what they need on behalf of their child."

Anita said, "Public school education stresses drill and skill. Their programs for kids with disabilities create systems around trying to educate the deficit rather than catering to the strengths of that child. British Primary School allowed us to investigate Kevin's strengths and build his educational confidence around them, filling in the spaces for the deficit with some very specific, but non-stressed, support."

"I think you've just defined the appropriate approach for the education of all kids with disabilities in this country," I said.

"I loved how they taught Kevin to read at British Primary," Jim said. "Instead of dealing with an alphabet, they taught word concepts. Kevin does know the individual letters because he can write them, but his overall approach to reading is based on meaning."

Anita said, "Remember the phrase 'Life is not a dress rehearsal'? The special-education system is a place where we tell our kids, 'You need to stay here and practice in order to gain the skills to live.' But then when they get out, they have spent all that time practicing, but not really living. British Primary said, 'Kevin, this is what you do well. You're wonderfully imaginative. We think you're great at block building.' Every time Kevin built a structure out of blocks and wanted to communicate 'Don't wreck my building' to the other kids, he was encouraged to write out a sign that said 'Don't wreck my building.' In this manner, Kevin's skills were driven forward based on his own desire to achieve. The teachers nurtured his passion for learning in that setting."

"Boy, you've hit my fundamental life issue," I said. "I am so focused on the need for people to be passionate. I think it's the quality that's lacking in many of us, so I'm glad to understand that Kevin found some passion. He has stayed in this wonderful setting through fifth grade. Now he's thirteen and you're facing the sixth grade. I bet we come back to the need to make another creative decision."

"That's right, Tom," Anita said. "I looked at schools in the community. The middle schools in the Denver area are traditional and would not meet Kevin's experiential needs."

"So what did you do?" I asked.

Jim said, "We found out that the only place Kevin could get what he needed was outside our county, in a unique, nontraditional public school. But there were no kids with disability in this setting."

"So how did you get Kevin in?"

Anita laughed. "I just walked into the school and met a wonderful teacher named Mike Delaney. I told him about Kevin, but I saved the part about Down syndrome till the last. He wasn't even shocked. He said, 'This is such an interesting conversation. We need more diversity in our school. I've always felt that this would be a great place for kids with disabilities, not just for them, but because the school community would be incomplete without this kind of diversity.

"'We do have a problem, though,' he added. 'We have an amazing waiting list. But please put Kevin's name on the list. Maybe we can move him up; we can sell the idea that he has special needs, and those needs could be met here.'

"By the end of summer, I had developed an aggressive letter-writing campaign. I asked teachers, friends, and others who knew Kevin well, to send in letters talking about who he was, and what their experience with his inclusion had meant to them.

"But the principal was quite hesitant. She feared that the needs of children in her own county might not be met if Kevin took up classroom space and extra support staff during his academic day. I persisted. Kevin had a chance to visit the school and spend a day in the classroom. All the teachers really liked him and Mike Delaney really lobbied for him. So in the end, we got him in."

"But, Anita, I still don't understand how you were able to get his IEP to agree to let him cross county lines."

Jim said, "Colorado law allows open enrollment on a space-available basis. And so, that's what we did."

"Jim, you make it all sound so simple, and I know that's not the case. Do you believe you had to pay a price to win the war?"

"I don't mean to sound too sappy," Jim replied, "but you've met Kevin. Don't you think those victories were worth the price?"

My response was obvious, so I asked, "What do you think the future holds for Kevin?"

"We don't know," Jim said, "but we're not going to have it limited by systems. We're going to watch while Kevin becomes all that he can be. If he finds his limits, it will be because those are his limits, not because they're imposed on him by the system."

Anita went on. "Kevin must define himself by his abilities, not be confined by his disability."

"Folks, I love that phrase, but how would you say Kevin is doing socially?"

Jim said, "That's the tough question. He grew up in a wonderful community where kids have come to know him over time. Because of that, he has been as included as was possible.

But he's coming to an age where we may begin to see separation. He's a teenager now and we have begun to feel that his interests, or maybe I should say, the interests of other young people, are not following the same track."

Anita put her head in her hands and I could hear the concern in her voice. "The most painful situation I've ever had to watch was Kevin phoning friends on a Saturday morning, not knowing if he'd find anyone to spend the day with him."

I reached across the coffee table and took both of their hands. "I'm so sensitive about this," I said, "because that was what my life was like. I used to hope the kids would want to play with me. It's a horrible feeling when you hear the rejection on the other end of the phone. I guess you just have to keep working day to day and appreciate those breakthroughs when they come."

"Tom, I know that there are gaps, and there will continue to be gaps between Kevin and his peers. It's our job to find ways to bridge those gaps and to ensure Kevin's inclusion in his own peer group."

"Anita, I believe that with the support of his family, Kevin can keep the gap closer than most kids."

It was time for me to head for the airport and fly back to California. When I thought about the factors that had made my life special, it seemed to me that my success had been based on the commitment of my mother, the uncompromising attitude of freedom provided by my father, the absolute love of my sisters, and the commitment of teachers and other professionals who lovingly encouraged me to be the best that I could be, along with an internal spirit that demanded I participate as an equal with others. That is a spirit that I know is shared by all of the children in this book.

I ordered a drink with dinner as I flew over the Rocky Mountains and found myself reflecting back on the six families that I had so come to love and respect over the last eight months while spending time on this work. How could I possibly put into words what I felt about them? But that's the dilemma of every author who writes a last chapter.

CHAPTER

Where the Roads Come Together

I BEGAN THIS BOOK with the story of my mother's revelations about her life as the parent of a blind child. Shocked by the extent of her pain and by the complexity of her experience in raising me, I embarked upon an eight-month journey, talking to parents who have children with disabilities in order to find out how much they share, linked by loving commitment.

From New England to California, with stops in Texas and Colorado, I believe my modest survey covers the spectrum of disability. By looking at cerebral palsy, blindness, a life-threatening illness, deafness, learning disability, and Down syndrome, we touch a wide range of issues and concerns affecting parents of all disabled children. Some people might criticize my selections (for example, I have only one girl and five boys in our profile), but I feel my representation is appropriate. The strength of this work is in the fact that my sampling is somewhat random. I did not go to organizations for the disabled to pick out their "showpiece" families. Rather, I chose those whom I knew or who became known to me through friends who were aware that I was working on this project.

That these human beings come through their challenges as remarkable people is a testimony to the quality and commitment of families throughout this country who are coping with the issue of raising children with disabilities. They teach us that courage can be found in all of us, when fate puts us in certain situations that force us to make difficult choices. As you have seen in the lives of our families, choices have always been made on the side of love. I like to believe that human beings are better than we might think, and that difficult circumstances can bring out the best in people. Here, that premise holds true.

Still, there are significant differences in the lives of our subjects. Anita and Jim Wagner, the parents of Kevin, our child with Down syndrome, had no time to know their son as a growing little person before his disability was thrust on them. In dealing with Jason's leukemia, Diana faced life and death rather than a specific disability (she has also been a single parent throughout much of Jason's life). All of our families have sibling situations with the exception of Nick and Lindy, who chose to raise Sean as an only child. Nevertheless, it is tremendously exciting for me to discover the extraordinary similarities between all of these families. And so, without retelling the stories, because no one could tell them as well as they did, I'd like to re-examine the road map of common issues suggested in chapter one.

COMMON GROUND

All of our parents found it difficult to communicate with their obstetricians and pediatricians in the early stages of their children's lives, and they all believed that this was because of the physicians' discomfort in imparting painful medical information. In some cases, the prognosis was inappropriate and misleading, as when the Jokelas were told that Cosmo might have a *slight* hearing loss. The boy was deaf. Kevin Wagner's pediatrician could have communicated the difficult reality of Down syndrome to his parents far more humanely. Lindy and Nick believe that they could have prepared more effectively for their future if their doctor had been more open in explaining Sean's problems. All of our parents, with the exception of the Wagners, went home believing that they had a normal child and began a painful process of figuring out what was wrong.

I was so moved hearing the families talk about this early period when denial is replaced by reality. Their experiences are amazingly similar. Fathers seem to deal with the truth earlier and more pragmatically than mothers, even though in time the day-to-day care of the child becomes the dominant factor in the mother's existence. Bob Rosso was very clear that he understood Jimmy was blind long before Robin did. Arthur Jokela had no doubt that Cosmo was deaf, months before Karen accepted it. Jim Wagner believed it was important to recognize that he and Anita had not had a perfect child, but could still do the best possible job with the child they had. Parents always hope for a totally healthy child, and it is their recognition that they do not have a perfect baby that causes so many of them to withdraw into a state of denial.

However, hope is an amazing part of the human character, and all of our parents clung to it. Karen clapped her hands behind Cosmo's head, hoping he would hear the sound. Robin

Rosso believed that her next-door-neighbor's little girl was an expert on blindness. Lindy allowed her parents to convince her that Sean was simply a colicky baby. And even Cheri and David Hartman, with all of their professional knowledge, chose to believe that Jeanie would simply outgrow her learning disability.

Without exception, all of the parents searched as quickly as they could for answers, and all of them made numerous false starts while trying to understand what was possible for their child. It seems that these families did not gain much from reading the literature. Anita Wagner noted that very little up-to-date information was available about children with Down syndrome. Others found that the books on blindness and deafness were not "self-help" or "how-to" manuals, but biographies of people like Tom Sullivan and Helen Keller.

All of our parents faced a critical turning point in their lives. For Lindy and Nick, it was the neurologist's confirmation that eighteen-month-old Sean had cerebral palsy. For Bob and Robin, it was the confrontation with the radiologist who diagnosed Jimmy's blindness. Diana listened to the doctor telling her that Jason quite likely had a death sentence hanging over his head. For Karen Jokela, something as simple as a bursting balloon was the moment of truth. The Wagners confronted the question of Kevin's disability at birth, but they, too, faced the pain of having to come to terms with the immensity of the problem. Anita's candid telling of her nightly hopes that Kevin might not wake up confirms the pain she must have felt. And the Hartmans anguished as they tried to frame a relationship between what they knew in their hearts and what they were able to deny with "professional mumbo jumbo."

A central concept takes over in the lives of these families at this critical moment. It is as complex as life, and as simple as survival. Parents must come to terms with the questions "Who is my child?" and "Will this life be framed by disability or defined by ability?" Successful adults who are coping with handicaps always define themselves as people first, with disability being only one part of the whole person. Parents of disabled children must learn to see their child like this to become successful, happy parents.

Parents arrive at this perspective in different ways. Some of them are guided by professionals who touch their lives, while others, like the Wagners, are moved by those who reach out with comments that reshape their beliefs. Jim and Anita Wagner's friends helped them understand that "God doesn't make junk," and this clearly began a healing process that has allowed them to give Kevin the support to live a rich and wonderful life.

Parents must also become champions for their children. This arises out of necessity and finds its voice when parents begin to fight for the children they love. The combination of love and necessity creates focused anger, and this release of intense energy channels these parents and helps them create possibilities for their children. I described Robin Rosso as a revolutionary, and she defined herself as a soldier on the front lines, fighting for her child to secure life's beachhead.

Is this overdramatizing an idea? I don't think so. It is at the parent's all-important turning point that the child's future begins to come into focus. Parents must always allow their sense of what is possible for their children to win over the perception that others have of them. It is they who must set the tone if the child with a disability is to be effectively nurtured. Because this is at odds with the world, they will be led to another important realization: They will come to understand that once they have accepted the disability, the day-to-day processes required to raise these special kids will force them to be so involved that they are in some ways insulated, even isolated, from the world at large. They do the best they can with the circumstances they are given, and literally take each day as it comes.

I was surprised at how truly isolated these parents are, even from their own families, while finding ways to deal with the problems of their special children. I am close to Lindy Allen's relatives, and I know how much they love her, yet it is clear to her that though they are totally committed to the idea that Sean can grow as a successful person, they do not have an effective grasp of the complexities surrounding his life as a child with cerebral palsy.

Often special parents can only find emotional and practical support from friends or other parents who have similar circumstances. All of us need people living in common circumstances in order to gain the strength to move forward and struggle for the success of the children we love.

Many have found people like this in parent coalitions. I am committed to the concept of parent-based organizations, but I aggressively recommend that parent groups enlarge their focus from a single disability to a universal parent approach that encompasses all of the organizations relating to Special-Needs children. Through this common approach parents will finally create truly inclusive environments for their children. I believe that whether it is from friends or professionals, parents need to find connections to possibilities in order to envision a pathway to success.

All of our parents suffered profound disappointments. Robin placed her faith in Jimmy's first teacher, who was more interested in knitting than listening to Lois Harrell speak on blindness. Lindy and Nick dealt with insensitive surgeons who seemed to have no interest in Sean, but only in the mechanics of their surgical technique. Diana coped with the arrogance of a doctor who was flippant with her during a life-and-death crisis.

These parents are constantly evaluating the help they get from friends and professionals, and trying to determine whether the associations and advice are beneficial. This is when parents first must begin to use their instincts. I call instinct the human ability to blend knowledge and experience to formulate appropriate (usually instantaneous) decisions. Parents should never doubt their basic instincts when raising their Special-Needs children. Diana Thomas believed for months before Jason was diagnosed with leukemia that something was gravely wrong. Robin Rosso was sure the information she was given by professionals, who were determining whether Jimmy was visually or mentally handicapped, couldn't be correct. All of the parents I interviewed believe absolutely that instinct is the single most important quality a parent must have, and trust, when raising a child with a disability.

While instinct seems to be the universal requirement for success in raising special children, the socialization process is without question the most complex. From birth, a child with a disability can never escape a painful reality. Everything the child does will be judged by others against the backdrop of his or her handicap, even while parents and children are constantly working to frame perception and define social interaction. My heart was broken when I heard Anita Wagner recount how Kevin called his friends on Saturday mornings, hoping that a child would agree to play with him. I remember days like those as if they were yesterdays. The disability heightens the social awkwardness every child feels and leads to individual isolation.

As I speak of being broken-hearted when learning about Kevin Wagner's predicament, I should also note that his social interactive skills are remarkable. From the joy he experiences skiing on Winter Park Mountain in Colorado, to the two summer jobs he now maintains, the Wagner family is truly socializing this wonderful young man. But the problem goes far beyond something as simple as being awkward. With many disabilities, there seems to be what I call "the social glitch." I believe this occurs when parents and professionals do not create social situations with peer groups on the child's behalf. A healthy self-image can never be dominated by a person's disability, and supportive social situations can draw attention toward the "whole person."

Parents must be willing to accept social failures with the belief that the child's desire to be interactive will overcome the pain of social rejection. That is certainly what Anita and Jim have chosen to do about Kevin. Parents must be inventive in their creation of opportunities for social interaction, and they must build their approach around the child's personal strengths. Jim Rosso is musical, so Robin and Bob are hard at work creating a musical environment that brings other like-minded children into interactive participation with him. Sean Allen loves sports, and even though cerebral palsy limits his ability to play baseball, Nick and Lindy are finding ways for him to enjoy the game he loves. The world is diverse enough so that children with disabilities can overcome social glitches and find appropriate placement in peer group interaction.

Siblings are the most important relations in the life of a person with a disability. To be the sibling of a Special Child can be either a person's greatest joy or a horrible burden that weighs heavy for the rest of one's life. Since the demands placed on parents of children with disabilities are so consuming, the attention given to siblings is generally inadequate, and siblings are often expected to understand the special needs of their brother or sister.

My sister Peggy was constantly forced to be more responsible than her friends, as she baby-sat and nurtured her blind brother. Mars Jokela's feelings that Cosmo's birth was the worst day of his life certainly is an exaggeration, and has now changed with the passage of time. But he pointed out that siblings can be burdened with a disability as great as the disabilities carried by their handicapped brothers and sisters. Parents must always remember the needs of their non-disabled children.

But when reflecting on the pressures these families faced, I believe the greatest is applied to the parents themselves. How can they maintain their individuality when the disability so dominates their time and their love? Lindy talked passionately about the loss of her identity while raising Sean, and how that affected her relationship with Nick. Only now with the help of outside sources for relief has this couple begun to share the kind of intimacy necessary to keep a marriage alive.

All of our parents speak of marital tension, and national statistics point to the scope of the problem. Depending on the surveys selected, between 65 and 72 percent of all families coping with disability face the pain of divorce.

Parents need to remember that they are individuals who fell in love with each other before they had a child with a disability. They must find ways to hold on to each other. They must treat each other with large doses of respect and love when times are difficult. They must find outlets for their uniqueness so that they are not just seen as the mother or father of a disabled child. They must find ways to create quality time that is sometimes shared and sometimes even enjoyed separately. Friendships must be cultivated and relationships outside the sphere of disability encouraged.

I am sure this is much easier said than done, but it must be done. A family coping with disability cannot survive if their individual lives are too narrow.

In all families, mothers and fathers take on different roles to facilitate family development. As I noted, in the case of families with disabilities, fathers tend to solve the immediate, practical issues since they seem to grasp the reality first. Nick dealt with Sean's medical problems, while Lindy coped with the educational and psychological side of raising a child with cerebral palsy. Bob Rosso chose to work on Jim's physical and mobility skills as a practical way of trying to promote Jim's participation with his peer group. Fathers tend to be solution-based and need to feel that they are involved in tasks that have immediate and measurable results. This male approach allows the mother to work for the child's social and educational life. When families apply themselves in this way, the child gains the best, most loving structure to facilitate his or her development.

It is in the arena of education that parents of children with disabilities fight their most intense battles. Here the issue of labeling becomes dynamic. Systems and good intentions, biases and bureaucracies, get jumbled in a Gordian knot that only committed parents can cut through. We have seen how our parents endured many educational crises. A corral was built around Sean's desk to isolate him from other kindergartners, and his wheelchair was placed at the end of the school parade, causing even more attention to be drawn to his disability. The Rossos were forced to send Jimmy away to school in another part of the state, placing him on an airplane every weekend. The pain must have been unbearable. Many of Jason Thomas's peer group thought that his leukemia was contagious, and they isolated him as a pariah. The Jokelas moved three times in order to provide Cosmo with an effective education. Cheri Hartman went to classroom after classroom only to be faced with antiquated systems, always wondering if this was all that was available for her special Jeanie. And the Wagners had to leave the public school system entirely in order to find an effective education for Kevin.

Even the children expressed their displeasure at their school situations. Jeanie Hartman and Kevin Wagner cried at the thought that they would have to return to their kindergarten classes, while Cosmo Jokela stopped his mother from signing during their first experience in school, knowing it was inappropriate.

All of the parents agreed that the most critical factor in their child's education was the development and implementation of an appropriate IEP, an Individual Education Plan. All of them have had to do this, and all of them have struggled with it. To be fair to the system, none of our parents have offered effective alternatives when it came to the discussion of the IEP. They accept the necessity of an organized approach for their child's education, but all agree that the IEP is generally handled too quickly and that there are too many people involved. The conversations within the IEP meetings should be structured far more toward reinforcing the child's abilities rather than facilitating his or her disabilities. More than anything else, the parents of a Special-Needs child must feel that those involved in the IEP process are truly interested in nurturing their youngster's education.

Parents must also take the time to learn about educational alternatives. Based on my experience as a person with a disability and the interviews I have conducted, I am convinced that the system is not meeting the needs of every child with a disability. However, I am also convinced that if parents know what's available, they can fulfill their child's academic requirements. It comes down to this: Parents must be leaders. They must move the process forward. They must define their child's future, recognizing that the system has most of what their children need to become successful adults. Lindy told me that in her IEP meeting, no one came prepared to lead, and she was forced to take on the responsibility for the development of an effective program. Sadly, some kids inevitably get placed on inappropriate tracks. Jimmy Rosso was wrongly labeled MH (multi-handicapped) rather than VH (visually handicapped). It was unclear whether Jeanie Hartman was learning-disabled or was dealing with Attention Deficit Disorder. Kevin Wagner is a child who has Down syndrome, but the system labeled him as "learning disabled" and "language delayed." Educators perceive cerebral palsy as a multiple handicap, limiting Sean Allen's appropriate classroom exposure.

I feel it's important for me to say to parents that though the system of educating children with disabilities is not yet perfect, it's come a long way since my mother and father fought the battles for a blind child forty years ago. Effective legislation and a much more enlightened society have greatly expanded the possibilities for every child with a disability to live a far more independent and fulfilled life.

My Turn

In these pages you have read remarkable stories, and though this is in every way a book designed to help parents speak to parents, I feel compelled to deliver some commentary of my own. The issues complicating the lives of these parents are formidable and endless. Their day-to-day struggles to turn a disability into an ability so that their children can live normal lives is almost unfathomable. It is frightening to recall the insensitivity of some professionals, both medical and educational, when dealing with the issues of Special Children. On the other hand, this book is also full of individuals whom parents see as truly special—people who have touched their children and made a difference.

Our parents must be people of unlimited energy—people who cannot ever allow their spirits to be broken by a system that so often seems insensitive. Despite their difficulties, they have found ways to define a central focus on behalf of their children. It is said that love sustains, and this work is a testimony to that fundamental belief.

The educational system is imperfect, but we have moved from the isolation of children with disabilities to mainstreaming, and now to an important concept that holds the greatest potential for Special Children—"inclusion." Inclusion of those children in our educational system and in our lives must be the goal of every parent and every professional. However, passing appropriate legislation does not guarantee success. The federal law 94/142, recently amended to be called IDEA (Individuals with Disabilities Education Act), has protected the rights of students with disabilities. But creating the least-restrictive environment for the education of a child with special needs can be challenging, not only for children but also for educators.

I also want to caution both parents and educators to recognize that the needs of Special Children may not always be met in a traditional educational environment. State schools for children with disabilities along with privately funded programs for Special-Needs children are critical supports for providing those extra elements that many of these children need to be educationally and emotionally fulfilled.

The goal is that the system will recognize the significance of inclusion and continue to expand boundaries in order to find a bridge between special needs and structural requirements. I think Anita Wagner said it best when she spoke of educating the *strengths* of children with disabilities and not overreacting to the challenges they represent.

Parents must be willing to rock the boat, to shake up systems, to be revolutionaries, because the battles they fight are for the most important people in their lives—their special children. The danger here is coming across as always confrontational. I want to emphasize that there are wonderful professionals working in the system. Many of them are overworked and underpaid. Parents must constantly reach out to find the best on behalf of their children—what Robin Rosso called the "A" list people. In all of our stories, the best was available, but the search was complicated.

I wrote this book because we are at a crossroads in our thinking about the future of children with disabilities. Our educational consciousness about disability is higher, but our budgets are being reduced. Our system is more sensitive, but far more overburdened by numbers and bureaucracy. We are saying all the right things, but there are too many important demands on education choking and slowing it down. Our committed professionals are so overstressed that they can easily lose their ability to think of each child individually. Unfortunately, none of the parents interviewed talked about receiving positive direction from educational authorities on behalf of their children. The capable people are obviously inside the system but generally not running it.

So what does this leave the parent? I suppose what has always been left to a parent—the sole responsibility for the care and development of their special children. The parents must first educate themselves, and then they have to carry forward, never accepting "No" when "Yes" is right for their child. They must form alliances when they find them, and they must come to that delicate balance between pushing the system forward and compromising, so that the situation in which their children find themselves doesn't return to the Dark Ages.

Parents must make up for what disability took away. It has always been like that, it will always be the same. The structure in which parents now find themselves has changed. But no longer is it enough to be the parent of a child who is blind, or a child who is deaf, or a child with cerebral palsy, or a child with Down syndrome, or a child with learning disability, or even a child who is ill. The parent of a child with a disability must now become the parent of all children with disabilities. These families have shown us the common ground that we all share. It is my great hope that you will use this information to move the entire system forward, not just segment it into individual camps based on individual disabilities.

When I began writing, I chose to call this book *Special Parent, Special Child,* but it wasn't until now that I truly understood the significance of the word *special.* The biblical quote "Many are called, but few are chosen" applies to these parents. For behind every disabled child who has a life of loving balance, there is a parent who has struggled to maintain that balance. It is difficult to be the parent of any child in the nineties, but the parents interviewed here have served as a testimony to the unique strength of those called to loving service on behalf of the Special-Needs children they so intensely nurture.

I very much thank these special families for allowing me to enter their lives so intimately, and I hope they will be proud to share the authorship of these pages with me for the sake of their children, and for all families who may benefit from their experience.